LITTLE WOMEN

LITTLE WOMEN

Adapted by Rachael Claye

MENSCH

Mensch Publishing

Mensch Publishing
51 Northchurch Road, London N1 4EE, United Kingdom

First Published in Great Britain 2020

ISBN: PB: 978-1-912914-07-4

Typeset by Van-garde Imagery, Inc., • van-garde.com

Contents

Cast List

(ages on first appearance)

MEG MARCH, 19

JO MARCH, 18

BETH MARCH, 16

AMY MARCH, 15

MA MARCH, a midwife in her late 40s

LAURIE LAURENCE, 18, Canadian

JOHN BROOKE, 25

DR JOHANN BHAER, 26

LITTLE WOMEN

Act 1, Scene 1

The March family living room on Christmas Eve. At one end of the traverse is a beaten-up four-seater sofa covered in present-wrapping detritus, cushions etc. On the floor is **Jo**'s *typewriter, with her scarlet writing hat prominently on top and papers scattered around it. The fairy lights have been set out but won't turn on – something is broken. A curious homemade artwork that might be a tree is half decorated. There is also a small wooden box in which the family place their Christmas wishes.*

Pre-show music plays as the audience comes in ('Next to Me' by Sleeping at Last), while **Meg** *tidies the room and sets* **Amy** *to decorate the tree. Eventually* **Meg** *calls* **Beth** *to help with the fairy lights. Music fades once the audience is settled.*

Meg OK. Gammon: in the oven. Presents: wrapped. Turkey: stuffed ready for tomorrow. Pigs: in their blankets. Veg: in a box in the garden. Lights: Beth. Tree ... whatever Amy is doing to the tree. Ma. On her way home. Oh God! Bread sauce. It's OK. Jo's getting bread sauce. Jo. Jo. Where is Jo?

Amy Where do you think?

Jo *bursts in wearing a fake Santa hat and beard, carrying shopping bags.*

Jo (*as* Santa) Ho ho ho! Merry Christmas!

Amy Every year...

Meg Where have you been?

Jo (*as* Santa) Why I've been circumnavigating the globe! Up and down chimneys, tending to the reindeer, you know, Rudolph ... the rest of them...

Act 1

Jo *hides the shopping bags behind the sofa.*

Meg Shopping? Jo, it's Christmas Eve! Have you wrapped anything at all?

Jo (*as Santa*) Of course not! I have my little helpers!

Amy No chance.

Meg Don't look at me. I still have to finish the cake.

Beth I can help.

Meg Beth, I need you to fix the lights.

Jo (*as Jo, to Beth*) But I'm rubbish at wrapping! Please?

Beth (*whispers*) I'll help you later.

Meg Did you get the bread sauce?

Brief pause.

Jo (*as Santa*) No! I forgot!

Meg Jo!

Jo (*as Jo*) I'm sorry, ok! Don't get mad. Please. Look, I remembered the most important thing – Ma's present.

She holds an envelope. They gather round it, excited.

Amy It doesn't look like much...

Jo It's what's inside that counts.

Amy *takes out a voucher.*

Amy Jo...

Meg *takes it.*

Meg This is way more than we said!

Jo   If you're going to do a thing, you may as well really do it.

Meg   You haven't used your savings? How are you ever going to get away to university?

Jo   I'll earn some more, it's no big deal.

Meg   It'll worry Ma.

Jo   Then I'll tell her not to worry.

Meg   Good luck with that.

Beth   I think it's lovely.

Pause.

Jo   (*as Santa, to* **Meg**) I'm sorry about the bread sauce.

Meg   I forgive you. One less thing to worry about.

Meg *starts clearing up.*

Jo   Is that your tree, Amy?

Jo *looks over* **Amy**'s *artistic interpretation of a Christmas tree.*

Amy   You hate it don't you.

Jo   I don't! It's really ... striking. It must have taken ages.

Amy   Beth helped.

Jo   Which bit did you do, Beth?

Beth   I made it.

Amy   To my design – I did all the decoration.

Meg *is clearing up the papers around* **Jo**'s *typewriter.*

Meg   What is this—

Jo   (*snatches*) Nothing.

Meg   A new story?

Beth   Can I read it?

Jo   Not till it's finished.

Amy   Is it about us?

Jo   It's going to be a lot more exciting than us.

Meg   (*finding wax on the floor*) Is this wax? Why can't you use electricity like a normal person?

Jo   Electricity has no magic.

Amy *has put* **Ma**'*s present under the tree. Distant piano music plays* (*'Sun, Instrumental' by Sleeping at Last*). **Beth** *goes to the window.*

Beth   Listen.

Amy   It's the new neighbours. They have a grand piano.

Beth   Whoever plays is really good.

Jo   Can't be the old scary one...

Amy   He's *called* Mr Laurence. And the young one is his grandson. And they are from *Canada*!

Jo   How do you know?

Amy   Their post came here and Ma took it round. And it *is* a palace.

Jo   Ma didn't say that...

Meg   It looks like a palace.

Jo   This is Crouch End. We don't have palaces.

Beth   I think he looks sad.

Jo   You would with only a bad-tempered old man for company.

Amy And a private tutor – the man in the *cardie*! Apparently, his grandfather is making him take his A levels again so he can be a lawyer.

Jo What a doom. I think we should rescue him.

Amy If I'm ever living in a house like that, don't bother rescuing me.

Jo *suddenly ducks down.*

Jo Oh no!

Amy Who is it?

Jo Keep out of the window, Amy!

Amy *has a good gawp.*

Amy Why are you hiding from Aunt March?

Jo Please – I *can't* see her...

Amy Well she's seen me and I refuse to be rude.

Jo I'm not here – make an excuse – don't ruin Christmas, Amy.

Amy I'm going down.

Amy *goes.*

Meg (*pointedly asking no questions*) Without Aunt March's help we wouldn't be in this house, Ma couldn't have finished her training—

Jo Don't we know it!

Beth Did you fall out with Aunt March?

Jo You betcha. There I was painting her rotten pantry – I bet Aunt March's ancestors kept slaves...

Meg   She's paying you.

Jo   Only just. Anyway, lucky old me in she squeezes to deliver a lecture. (*Parroting Aunt March*) 'One A star, a D and an E Josephine – it's hardly going to be Oxbridge.'

Beth   She didn't say that.

Meg   What did you say?

Jo   Plenty.

Amy *enters with painting overalls which she gives to* **Jo**. **Beth** *gets back to fixing the lights.*

Amy   Wow, Jo.

Jo   (*sarcastic*) 'Happy Christmas, Jo!' Is she gone?

Amy   What's that word like a candle exploding but it means really cross?

Meg   What?

Jo   Err ... incandescent!

Amy   Exactly. She actually said she washed her hands of you.

Jo   Not before I wash mine of her!

Meg   Can't you ever keep your temper?

Jo   I don't see eye to eye with her and she may as well know it.

Amy   I think she does.

Meg   But Jo, it was a job...

Beth   Maybe the shoe shop would take you back?

Amy *and* **Meg** *exchange a glance – not likely.*

Jo   What? I was sacked for being honest!

Meg   Maybe you really should think about teaching.

Jo   I'm not that desperate.

Meg   At least you can get on a scheme.

Amy   Teaching is what people do when all hope is gone.

Meg   That's harsh.

Amy   You've forgotten what school's like.

Jo   Well I look on this as a blessing. I'll make my own way – I'll take the loans and work at whatever job I can get and go to University and read literature and then I'll write a bestseller and pay off the lot. Who knows what opportunities will open up now Aunt March has been blasted by the bright sunlight of pure feeling!

The fairy lights come on.

Meg   Beth, you did it!

Amy   They look fab.

Jo   Right, now it's Christmas! Amy, put some music on. Meg, put your feet up. Beth. Dance with me.

Music plays ('Taste – Instrumental' by Sleeping at Last) as **Jo** *swings* **Beth** *round and* **Amy** *and* **Meg** *join in. They collapse on top of* **Beth** *on the sofa.* **Ma** *enters.*

Ma   What in the world are you doing with that poor thing?

Jo   Celebrating!

Beth   I'm fine, Ma.

Ma Of course *you* are – I meant the sofa. It won't last another day.

Meg Happy Christmas Eve, Ma.

Ma Everything looks lovely, Meg.

Amy Come and see my tree!

Ma Well. That is quite ... something. Well done, Amy.

Jo And Beth.

Ma And Beth.

Meg Come and sit down.

Ma I should write up my notes—

Jo No chance. Meg, get the whisky.

Beth I'll take your bag.

Jo Hide it, Beth.

Beth *brings a stool for* **Ma***'s feet.*

Beth How was your day, Ma?

Ma Well. Babies got themselves born and I involved myself.

Meg *brings* **Ma** *whisky.*

Amy Is it time now?

Jo Amy – she's just sat down!

Amy We've been waiting all day!

Ma I'm surprised you lasted that long.

Amy Can we open two?

Jo You know the rules.

Amy   You always say if you don't like rules then ignore them.

Ma   She means other rules.

Meg   You look tired.

Ma   I'm fine.

Jo   What's the haul?

Ma   Five pounder, a little girl. Ruby.

Beth   Ruby. That's a lovely name.

Jo   Is she alright?

Ma   Oh yes. Hannah took over from me, she's a safe pair of hands.

Pause.

Meg   What's up, Ma?

Ma   Nothing.

Jo   What sort of nothing?

Ma   Just … I don't know. Little Ruby … her mother is so young, she had nobody with her. I went to get a few things for her afterwards from her home.

Amy   Is that part of your job?

Ma   Taking good care of mothers and their babies, that's my job, Amy. Her place was freezing, no electricity, no food in the cupboard. I gave her a bit of cash – said it was to buy a gift for the baby.

Meg   Ma...

Ma   I know, I know. But Meg, a young mum like that, all on her own. It's the most precious trust there is. You can't let your children down.

Meg   You've never let us down.

Ma   Come on. Let's not be sad. Amy, do you want to go first?

Amy   Thought you'd never ask!

Amy *gets a present from under the tree.*

Amy   From Meggie ... Yes! Sketchbook and pencils – are these the posh ones we saw in the window?

Meg   Yup.

Amy   Thank you!

Meg   Make good use of them.

Amy   I will – I'll sketch you all – the Mad Marches, captured for immortality by Amy March.

Beth   Meg next.

Beth *hands over a present.*

Meg   Aunt March.

Jo   Uh-oh.

Amy   Aunt March gives great presents.

Jo   To *you*. Do you remember that make-up set she gave me?

Amy   That was hilarious!

Jo   It was like we'd never met.

Meg   Something soft ... smallish ... hmm, something chic to wear? ... A rain mac.

Jo   See.

Beth   Jo, this one's from me.

Jo *unwraps a box.*

Jo   This is beautiful. Did you make it?

Beth   Yes.

Jo   Beth...

Beth   I know it's a bit plain. I thought you could keep your stories in it.

Jo   I will. Thank you. Now you!

Amy   I thought you said you hadn't wrapped anything.

Jo *winks at* **Meg** *and hands* **Beth** *a small, squishy present.*

Jo   (*joking*) It's a piano.

Beth   I wish.

Beth *opens it. Inside is a toy chicken.*

Beth   He's very ... sweet.

Jo   Looks a bit poorly – perhaps it needs some air – let's take it in the backyard...

Amy   What is she doing?

Meg   Go and see...

Jo *sends* **Beth** *through the door.* **Amy** *follows.*

Beth   (*calling from off-stage*) Chickens!

Beth *returns.*

Beth   You've actually got me real chickens!

Jo   What do you think?

Beth   They're gorgeous, I love them!

Amy   Meg, did you know about this?

Meg   I may have heard something.

Amy   Ma?

Ma   This was all Jo's idea.

Beth   The coop is great – I could build a bit on for them to roam.

Jo   What are you going to call them, Beth?

Amy   Itch and stitch. Ink and stink. Harold and Hilda.

Jo   They're female.

Amy   So?

Beth   I'm going to call the red one Spots and the greeny-black one Sparkle.

Meg   Come on, Ma, open yours.

Ma   I told you I didn't want anything.

Jo   It's only little.

Jo *hands* **Ma** *the envelope.*

Ma   It's a voucher. 'Wild Travel'. What is this?

Jo   It's your ticket to adventure, Ma.

Ma   The Northern Lights!

Meg   You always said you wanted to see them.

Jo   Everything's covered – all you have to do is hop on a plane and get off in Norway!

Amy   And ring up and book when you want to go.

Ma   This must have cost a small fortune.

Meg   You work so hard for us.

Ma   You're supposed to be saving up.

Amy   Me and Beth put in a bit too.

Beth   Is it alright, Ma?

Ma   It's ... wonderful. Just what I didn't know I needed. Thank you, darlings.

Jo   I'll put it on your desk so it doesn't get lost.

Meg   Is it time for the toast?

Beth   Wait. I want to change mine.

Beth *finds her piece of paper in the wishes box and writes something new.*

Amy   It's my turn this year!

Jo   You did it last year.

Amy   Beth gave me her turn so now it's my turn again.

Jo   That's not how it works.

Ma   Amy. It's Jo's turn.

Beth *hands* **Jo** *the box.* **Jo** *reads the family's wishes out one by one from scraps of paper as the others try to guess the writer.*

Jo   Dear Mad Marches, it is my honour this Christmas Eve to propose a toast in hopes of ... 'Success and recognition in our' ... I think that's supposed to say 'travails', though it actually reads 'travels'.

Meg   Amy.

Jo   'To find our feet, and not fall on our' ... there's some crossing out, does that say 'elbows'?

Beth Ma.

Jo 'To be glad of what we have, which is each other—'

Ma Beth.

Jo Not this time— 'because the rest of the world makes no sense at all'.

Meg Jo.

Jo 'To get a better job where I don't have to gift-wrap the same organic cotton babygrow seventy times.' Well, it's not Ma...

Meg *raises her hand ruefully.*

Jo And, finally, 'To take our gammon with toffee sauce up to the hospital, and share it with Ruby's new mum.'

Meg Beth...

Amy She's not serious, is she?

Meg We could...

Jo We really could.

Amy But it's our Christmas Eve meal! It's special.

Jo It's her Christmas too.

Beth We don't have to. I just thought it would be nice.

Amy There might not be enough.

Jo For Ruby's mum?!

Amy Everyone will want some!

Jo Good.

Meg We can take the cake too...

Beth   Really – can we do it? Do you mind, Ma?

Ma   I can't think of a better way to celebrate Christmas.

The girls run off over the following lines:

Meg   I need to sieve the sauce.

Beth   I'll help.

Jo   I'll watch.

Amy   (*reluctantly*) I'll carry the cake.

They go. **Ma** *looks up to the lights and makes a toast.*

Ma   (*to Michael*) Merry Christmas, Michael my love.

(*Transition music: 'Found Letters' by Sleeping at Last.*)

Act 1, Scene 2

The Laurence house next door. **Brooke** *is reading from a textbook while* **Laurie** *gazes out of the window.*

Brooke   (*reading*) 'The doctrine of manifold destiny recalls the Puritan John Winthrop's famous City Upon a Hill sermon of 1630...'

Brooke *sees that* **Laurie** *is not listening.*

Brooke   ...in which he urged a young and promising student not to fritter away his grandfather's money on lessons that aren't listened to, thereby wasting all of his advantages—

Laurie *laughs.*

Brooke   Laurie?

Laurie   Sorry.

Brooke Laurie, you're not unintelligent but if you don't try and concentrate—

Laurie She's gonna drop the gravy boat!

Brooke Who?

Laurie Nice save!

Brooke *looks despite himself.*

Brooke Who are they?

Laurie The girls from next door – you must have seen them.

Brooke Oh ... yeah.

Laurie *notices where* **Brooke**'*s eye falls.*

Laurie That one's called Meg.

Brooke She's got a lovely ... roasting pan?

Laurie They're always up to something.

Brooke Where are they taking it all...

Laurie Maybe we could lend a hand?

Brooke *drags his eyes away.*

Brooke We should get on.

Laurie Meg's the eldest...

Brooke Listen, Laurie, with your re-sits coming up, should you be spending quite so much time staring out of the window?

Laurie It's something to do with my eyes.

Brooke *holds up the textbook.*

Brooke This is something to do with your eyes.

Laurie   (*fatefully*) Oh yes.

Brooke Shall we?

Laurie   Back with you.

Brooke Great news.

Brooke (*reading*) 'In his sermon, John Winthrop urged the creation of a virtuous community in America to be a shining example to the Old World.' Would you read the next bit?

Laurie Sure.

Brooke *paces a little, working his way towards the window.*

Laurie   (*reading*) 'As one follower wrote in an influential pamphlet…'

Brooke *gazes from the window at Meg. Perhaps there is the suggestion of a smile or even a wave, which is seen by* **Laurie**.

Laurie   'The birthday of a new world is at hand!'

Laurie *snaps the book shut behind* **Brooke**.

(*Transition music: 'Taste, Instrumental' by Sleeping at Last.*)

Act 1, Scene 3

The March family living room. **Ma** *is writing up her clinical notes.* **Beth** *enters.*

Beth   Can I interrupt?

Ma   You and your endless demands, Beth! Come on, I'm ready.

Beth   Jo showed me this course they do at the technical college.

Ma   College…?

Beth   I know I said I didn't want to, but, now I'm not sure.

Ma   Well, tell me.

Beth   It's carpentry, but they have options – you can look at different kinds of mechanisms, clockwork, all sorts. They do one on musical devices. I know it's a bit old fashioned...

Ma   Sounds perfect. But?

Beth   It's a big college. Really big.

Ma   Doesn't mean there isn't a quiet corner for you.

Beth   Ma, I'm worried it'll be like school again – I'll be the one on their own who never speaks and no one wants to know.

Ma   You've the right to be yourself.

Beth   It doesn't feel like that. People think I'm strange. They don't understand.

Ma   The ones that are worth it will.

Beth   Ma, I rang up.

Ma   Good for you!

Beth   They said I should come in for a chat.

Ma   You can do that. It's just a couple of people in a room. They'll listen to you.

Beth   What if I can't speak...

Ma   Take the things you've made, talk about them.

Beth   If I dry up they'll think I'm an idiot.

Ma   Beth, you've as much right to learn as anyone. Let other people fill the air with nonsense. Don't think you're any the less. In my opinion you're far more.

Beth Do you really think?

Ma They'll be lucky to have you. If you have any trouble you just tell me. I'll put them straight.

Beth I can't rely on you forever.

Ma Yes you can! It's in my job description. Now, practice.

Beth What?

Ma Walking into the room. Up you get.

Beth (*reluctantly*) Alright...

Ma Now, I'm a teacher, not particularly unfriendly, I actually quite like young people. Who's this at my classroom door?

Beth It's me, Beth.

Ma Beth March. How lovely to meet you. And what are all these things you've brought?

Beth Just things I made.

Ma You must have an excellent teacher.

Beth I taught myself.

Ma You taught yourself? Impossible!

Beth I did.

Ma In all my years I have never met a young person with such skill. I don't know Beth, we may have to skip the course and give you a job teaching instead.

Beth Ma!

Beth *is laughing.*

Ma See, Beth? They'll love you. Who wouldn't?

We hear off stage shouts.

Meg   (*from offstage*) Ow, Jo be careful!

Jo   (*offstage*) Well stop moving.

Ma   Uh-oh.

Beth   What's going on?

Ma   Somehow, against all the odds, Meg has persuaded Jo to go to Sally Gardiner's New Year's Eve party – I know!

(*Transition music: 'Dancing on my Own' by Robyn.*)

Act 1, Scene 4

Club. **Meg** *and* **Jo** *lurk at the edge of a thronging crowd.*

Jo   I'm really—

Meg   Don't say anything.

Silence.

Jo   It's just I—

Meg   Much better if you don't.

Jo   Hair grows back.

Meg   Not within the hour.

Jo   Amy did an amazing cover-up job.

Meg   The best that can be said is, it's dark. And I will never trust you with curling tongs again.

Meg *waves to someone out of sight.*

Jo   Who's that?

Meg   Sally's brother – don't stare!

Pause.

Jo   When can we go?

Meg   Keep smiling. You owe me. He's cute. I think he's pointing at the bar...

Jo   You know you can't hold your drink.

Meg   I so can. Come on.

Jo   No way – it's you he wants to talk to.

Meg   Fine. Stay here. But remember, we said no mad dancing this time.

Jo   What am I – some kind of embarrassing parent?

Meg   He'll think my family are nuts.

Jo   Fine...

Meg *goes.* **Laurie** *and* **Jo** *bump into each other.*

Jo   Oh God! Sorry. Hi.

Laurie   Oh God sorry hi yourself.

Jo   I didn't think anyone else was lurking back here.

Laurie   That's me, invisibly lurking.

Jo   I'm Jo.

Laurie   Nice to meet you. I'm Laurie.

The shake hands with mock formality.

Jo   You literally live next door, don't you?

Laurie   So I do.

Jo   Hang on – Laurie Laurence?

Laurie Laurie's a nickname. You actually have the honour of addressing Theodore.

Jo   What – like Teddy?

Laurie It actually means 'gift of God', so...

Jo   What were your parents thinking?

Laurie I never knew them.

Jo   Oh, God, sorry.

Laurie There you go again.

Jo   I mean, I didn't mean, that's not funny. My father died too. I was only young. My Ma talks about him all the time.

Laurie Well, you have her.

Cringe moment for **Jo***.*

Jo   My sister loves your place.

Laurie Come over some time, I'll give you the tour.

Jo   I didn't mean – yeah, thanks.

Music plays ('Mr Brightside' by The Killers). **Jo** *checks to see if* **Meg** *is watching.*

Jo   Hey, do you want to dance?

Laurie Thought you'd never ask.

Laurie *does a grand flourish. He and* **Jo** *dance wildly. They collapse in giggles.*

Jo   You didn't learn those moves off your grandfather.

Laurie He's not the dancing type.

Jo So, it's just you and him in that big old house?

Laurie And my tutor, the lovely Brooke.

Jo Is he?

Laurie Brooke's not so bad. It's me – he talks American Civil War, my mind goes skittering off to ... I don't know.

Jo Where?

Laurie You'll laugh.

Jo Maybe I will. Tell me anyway.

Laurie Smokey jazz bars in New York.

Jo That's like my sister, Amy – she's got these big plans to be a great artist in Paris.

Laurie My grandfather calls it 'building castles in the air'. I've made about a hundred.

Jo Tell me one.

Laurie Er ... Berlin, a derelict warehouse, one vast room with windows from floor to ceiling, guitars, drum kits and a fabulous grand piano that I can play all day—

Jo So it is you we hear.

Laurie I guess so. What about you?

Jo I'm still hatching.

Laurie Come on, you can tell your kindly neighbour Teddy...

Jo Maybe I want to do something ... heroic!

Laurie Heroic?

Jo   Yes, why not? Something heroic and wonderful that won't be forgotten after I'm dead. I don't know what yet, but I'm on the watch, and one day, I will astonish you.

Laurie   Well, I'll drink to that.

He becomes mock formal.

Laurie   Hey, may I get mademoiselle something from the bar?

Jo   Water would be divine – all this dancing has me parched!

Laurie   At once.

Laurie *goes,* **Jo** *looks after him in amusement.* **Meg** *enters, limping.*

Jo   What's wrong?

Meg   Nothing.

Jo   It's those heels.

Meg   It's no big deal.

Jo   Meg, didn't I say...

Meg   Don't. Fuss.

Jo   How was it with Sally's brother – does he have a name?

Meg   Chris.

Jo   Chris. Nice ... chat?

Meg   Very nice actually.

Jo   Got a lot in common?

Meg   Enough. He asked if I'd like to come to a 21st at his friend's cottage in Wiltshire. It's a whole weekend. So, er, yeah, I'd say we got on.

Laurie *returns with water for* **Jo**.

Laurie There you go, mademoiselle – (*to* **Meg**) Hi. I'm Laurie.

Meg Oh ... Meg – Ow!

Laurie Can I get you something?

Jo Stretcher maybe.

Meg Don't listen to her. She's a massive exaggerator.

Laurie She's a fine dancer.

Meg Oh...? Really...?

Jo We should go.

Meg Oh, don't leave the fun just for me. Please continue dancing.

Jo Please continue walking.

Meg *lets out a cry of pain.*

Jo (*concerned*) Meggie...

Laurie I can give you a lift – I've got my car.

Jo *looks to* **Meg** *– she nods.*

Jo Thank you, Laurie. Hop along, Meg.

Jo *helps* **Meg**, *who smiles suggestively as* **Laurie** *goes.*

Jo Don't even think it.

Act 1, Scene 5

The March family living room. **Ma** *is writing up her notes at her desk. She stops to look at a photo of Michael.*

Ma   Oh Michael, the Northern Lights. When am I going to find time to fit them in? It's not that I don't crave adventure, though I don't. It's just that not being on an adventure is already exhausting. I think the girls may have forgotten. They're all taken up with this boy next door. *(She chuckles to herself.)* I mean, Laurie Laurence, poor kid! He's sweet – it's like having a Labrador puppy around. I've never known the girls take an outsider to their hearts like this...

Jumps to **Jo**, **Meg**, **Amy** *and* **Beth** *at home in top hats and pipes or other outlandish gear they have pulled from their childhood dressing up box, adopting a high style in line with their outfits.*

Jo   *(as literary delegate)* Madame president, delegates. I wish to propose a new member – one who deserves the honour, would be deeply grateful for it, and would add immensely to the spirit of the club and its literary value. I propose that Mr Theodore Lawrence be added to the roll.

Amy   Objection! He's a boy.

Meg   Sustained.

Jo   *(breaking out of role)* Oh go on!

Amy   A boy can't be in a society called the Fabulous Girls.

Jo   *(remembering herself)* I beg my literary friends' indulgence a moment. While we are, admittedly, a literary society for Fabulous Girls, I move that in this exceptional case the benefits of our society be extended to one who would dearly feel the joy of them. It is our privilege, is it not, to be inclusive, flexible, forward thinking, and occasionally silly.

Amy   Having a boy would spoil everything.

Jo   (*breaking role again*) That's so binary.

Meg   Order! Let's put it to the—

Jo   (*holding up her hand*) Aye!

Meg   —vote. All those in favour?

Jo   Aye!

Beth   Aye.

Meg   Those against?

Amy   No way.

Meg   Me neither.

Jo   What?

Meg   Boys make fun of you. They're terrible listeners and they take up all the space.

Jo   Not Laurie – he's nice and he makes me laugh.

Beth   It's unkind to leave him out.

Jo   Well said, Beth. (*Back in role.*) I call for a second referendum. He's been a friend to me and Meg, let's be friends back – and let not gender tear us asunder. All those in favour say aye!

Beth   Aye.

Meg   Aye ... ish.

Amy   Oh alright then.

Jo   Allow me to present our new member!

Laurie *bursts out from his hiding place.*

Meg   Jo, you total rotter.

Amy   Hi, I'm Amy.

Jo   This is Beth.

Laurie Pleased to meet you both.

Beth   Did you hear everything?

Laurie I did and greatly appreciate the honour of membership. I have prepared a small contribution to begin – ahem: 'There once were four maidens called March—'

Meg   I told you! Out!

They go. We return to **Ma**.

Ma   Jo has accepted an offer to study English – which seems to mean paying a lot of money to lie around reading novels. At least she'll stay here and not have to pay rent. A small gleam of practicality. I wish Meg would think about her future. She and Sally are thick as thieves. And now this party with Sally's brother – oh Michael, he's even more empty-headed than his sister.

Jumps to **Meg** *arriving in the drive of a huge house, carrying an overnight bag, looking upwards... and upwards.*

Meg   Cottage? This can't be it.

Meg *consults the directions.*

Meg   This is it. I'm about to enter a house with a turret.

Meg *prepares herself.*

Meg   I can do this. I can totally do this.

Meg *walks a little way up the drive.*

Meg   I can't do this.

Meg *is about to turn and flee but she sees someone at the window. She puts on a smile and waves enthusiastically.*

Meg   OK Meg March. Right.

Meg *pulls herself together and assumes a confident air.*

Meg   I can totally do this.

Meg *is head down and off up the drive.*

Meg   Oh shhhhhh...

Meg *goes. We return to* **Ma***.*

Ma   What kind of magic is it that creates confidence? I couldn't believe in Beth more than I do. I couldn't love her more. I wish I could carry her through those college doors in my arms and say to them – this is my daughter and she's fantastic. Just give her a chance, just ... listen to her. I hope they're kind.

Jumps to the road in front of college: **Beth** *is carrying a box of things she has made, head down, not looking at the door towards which she is advancing. She slows, she stops.*

Beth   Beth March. These are some things I made. I taught myself.

Beth *looks at the door. She pulls herself together and goes towards it.*

Beth   Beth March. These are some things I made. I taught myself.

Beth *stops.*

Beth   Beth March...

Beth *pauses. She walks abruptly away. We return to* **Ma**.

Ma   Oh – Amy! Our littlest, our loudest. I got the call from the school, *again*. This time Science. So off I had to trudge to Mr Radcliffe's office all because...

Jumps to **Amy**.

Amy   (*all in one breath*) I drew a cartoon of him instead of doing the questions but it was hardly anything but he said it was the 'final straw' so he made me stand in the Internal Exclusion Unit for two entire hours which is this room with glass walls where you have to sit on your own if you get into trouble and everyone can see in and you're not even allowed to take a book in, you have to sit there and think about what you've *done wrong* and Georgia Williams kept going past with her mates and staring at me and sniggering behind her hand. Argh!

Amy *goes. We return to* **Ma**.

Ma   I always hated Mr Radcliffe. 'There are better ways to discipline children than humiliating them.' That's what I said to him. Then I freed Amy from her prison and stormed out. Though of course as soon as we were outside I grounded her for a week. Well, that's about it for now. I keep teaching the lessons, but the learning they do for themselves–

Meg *enters*.

Ma   Darling, how was it?

Meg   Yeah really great fine thanks.

Ma   Oh. Good. You and Sally had a nice time together?

Meg   Great yeah.

Ma   Well. That is good news. I'll put the kettle on—

Meg   Actually me and Sally...

Ma   Yes?

Meg   We fell out. She leant me this really expensive dress and I spoilt it.

Ma   You can make it up to her I'm sure.

Meg   I made such an idiot of myself!

Ma   With Sally?

Meg   With everyone! Chris had this friend, Fred Vaughn, and I don't know what came over me but he got me into this stupid drinking game called (*deep breath*) 'Tufty Buffington' with forfeits and I suppose I was trying to impress everyone and he said bet you can't drink down a whole bottle of vodka—

Ma   Meg, that's dangerous.

Meg   Well it wasn't because it came straight back up.

Ma   Oh dear.

Meg   All down Sally's silk designer dress with the pantaloons.

Ma *tries not to laugh.*

Meg   It's not funny!

Ma   I'm not laughing.

Meg   I spent the whole night with my head down the loo throwing up, listening to Sally scrub her dress in the bath and crying except for when she was saying mean things to me and

I offered to pay to clean it properly but she says it's ruined and Chris and his friends didn't even say goodbye in the morning and I heard Fred Vaughn telling everyone Sally only hangs out with me to make herself look good.

Ma   Oh Meg, come here.

Ma *hugs* **Meg**.

Ma   This feeling will pass.

Meg   It was social death!

Ma   So what if it is. Do you know what a real friend is Meg? It's someone who values you higher than an outfit. Look at me – isn't it?

Meg   I suppose. Yes. I'm an idiot, aren't I?

Ma   You're lovely. Just learn from it.

Meg   I wish everyone was as sympathetic as you.

Ma   I've had professional training. Now, let's get a cup of tea down you. And next time, don't forget who you are because you're so busy trying to impress everyone else.

Meg   If I ever do, say one thing to me – Tufty Buffington!

They exit together.

Act 1, Scene 6

The March family living room. **Jo** *is alone, wearing her scarlet writing hat and tapping away on her typewriter.* **Laurie** *creeps in clutching his guitar but she's too absorbed to notice. He sneaks up behind and plays a sudden dramatic chord.*

Jo Laurie! Go...

Pause as **Jo** *is absorbed in what she is about to write.*

Laurie I'm sorry?

Jo ...away!

Laurie *punctuates his words with dramatic chords.*

Laurie The. Snow. Is. Falling.

No response. He tries again.

Laurie Outside!

Jo I'm busy.

Jo *pushes* **Laurie** *away.*

Laurie Neighbour abuse – Beth, save me!

Jo She's gone to see baby Ruby.

Laurie Wow – the maestra speaks.

Jo You said you'd be studying.

Laurie It's killing me. I'm dead inside.

Jo The dead are quieter.

Laurie Seriously, come out – even in prison they get breaks for good behaviour.

Jo   I'm on the last chapter – I'm so nearly there.

Laurie Brooke says Hampstead pond is freezing over...

Jo   You go.

Laurie Who are you and what have you done with Jo March, adventurer?

Jo   I'll join you when I'm done.

Laurie How long will that be?

Jo   As long as it takes.

Laurie *gives up.*

Laurie Can I study with you?

Jo   If you're quiet. Super quiet.

Laurie You won't notice me.

Jo *writes.* **Laurie** *carefully gets out notebook, pens etc. He freezes at every little noise, but fails to settle down to study.* **Jo** *gives up.*

Jo   Do you even like history?

Laurie *plays a tragic chord on the guitar by way of response.*

Jo   Then why study it?

Laurie I like grandfather.

Jo   If he loves you, he won't want you to be unhappy.

Laurie We've got different ideas about happy.

Jo   I guess it's hard being the only one.

Laurie *plays a sad little tune.*

Jo   Can't you tell him?

Laurie The old man spent his life building up a giant law firm. I'm all he's got left and I don't want it. How does one phrase that?

Jo *doesn't know. Perhaps* **Laurie** *elaborates his sad little tune.*

Jo I'm going to put you in my next story. The tale of the tragic lawyer.

Laurie Musician.

Jo The tragic musician.

Laurie Brilliant musician.

Jo Brilliant musician.

Laurie Brilliant successful musician!

Jo Whatever.

Laurie *plays the guitar excitedly.*

Jo What are we going to do with you?

Laurie Muck around.

Jo Long-term.

Laurie Pass. What are we going to do with you?

Jo Why don't you go out in the snow and I'll come and find you when I'm done, and we'll make snow people.

Jo *resumes writing.* **Laurie** *takes up his history book at last. Pause.*

Laurie Have you ever been to the opera?

Jo Of course not – is this quiet?

Laurie I just wondered if you'd like to go.

Jo I'm good thanks.

They resume their activities. Pause.

Jo OK, out with it.

Laurie It's grandfather's birthday.

Jo And?

Laurie His firm got him these fancy tickets to see Carmen at Covent Garden, only he doesn't have any friends, not real friends. All he does is work. There's me and there's his colleagues. And his colleagues don't seem to have the time, so...

Jo I suppose I could bring Meg – she loves that kind of thing.

Laurie You're a saint!

Jo But only if you take a vow of silence so I can write.

Laurie Total.

Pause.

Laurie Love you!

Jo Total vow!

Laurie Not another word.

Jo *resumes writing.* **Laurie** *tries to stay quiet.*

Laurie Maybe I'll see if Brooke's free too.

Jo Argh!

Jo *leaps up and chases* **Laurie** *out.*

Act 1, Scene 7

The March family sitting room: **Beth** *and* **Amy**. **Amy** *has been trying on outfits but nothing is right.*

Amy   Beth what do you think – edgy or dowdy?

Beth   You look nice.

Amy   Dowdy. I'll never get into A level art looking dowdy.

Beth   They'll look at your work.

Amy   It's the only decent sixth form college for art in North London – Georgia Williams is applying! I've got to ... can I borrow something of yours?

Beth   Do I look edgy?

Amy   You're right. It'll have to be ... Bethie, do me a favour?

Beth   Possibly.

Amy   Jo's leather jacket is on the back of the chair in her room. Could you get it for me?

Beth   Can't you go?

Amy   Please! She's in one of her writing moods and if I interrupt she'll get annoyed, but she always says yes to you.

Beth   You want me to ask her if you can borrow it?

Amy   Maybe just don't say that much – once I've tried it on I'll show her, just pop my head round the door and she won't be able to resist.

Beth   I'm not sure if—

Amy   Only just to try it – then I'll come clean. Promise. Please Bethie, please...

Beth   Just to try...

Amy   Just to try! It'll make such a difference.

Beth   And you'll definitely check with Jo.

Amy   Definitely. Please?

Beth *goes.* **Amy** *sorts pictures in her art portfolio.* **Beth** *returns with the jacket, deeply conflicted.*

Amy   You're an angel!

Beth   Jo thinks I've got a date.

Amy   What?!

Beth   She asked me what it was for. I panicked. I told her I was meeting someone.

Amy   You're kidding.

Beth   I can't believe I did that.

Amy   I can't believe she believed you.

Beth   She gave me a massive bear hug. Oh no...

Amy *puts on the jacket.*

Amy   Oh yes! I've got to go.

Beth   What about Jo?

Amy   Listen, the interview's half an hour, I'll be there and back before she's even noticed.

Beth   She'll think I lied. I did lie.

Jo *enters.*

Jo   Beth, I forgot to say, Laurie's got these tickets... What's this?

Amy   I've got my interview for sixth form.

Jo   That's mine – Beth?

Beth   I'm sorry.

Jo   Did you make Beth take my jacket?

Amy   You always assume the worst of me!

Beth   It's my fault, I took it.

Jo   She made you.

Amy   Beth has her own free will.

Jo   Give me my jacket back.

Amy   I need it – you can't do this – not just before my interview!

Jo   I so can.

Jo *snatches a picture from* **Amy**'s *art portfolio, holds it out of her reach and makes as if to tear it in two pieces.*

Jo   Swapses.

Amy   You. Wouldn't.

Beth   Jo I'm really sorry, this is all my fault.

Jo   It's Amy's fault, isn't it, Amy?

Amy   That's my sketch of Man with Guitar!

Jo   Not for long.

Amy   Jo!

Amy *pulls off the jacket and throws it to the floor.* **Jo** *lets the picture fall.*

Jo   Thank you.

Jo *puts on her jacket.* **Amy** *reassembles her art portfolio.*

Amy   You're horrible, Jo March.

Jo   Just trying to teach my little sister a few basic life lessons. Right. Beth, would you like to come out with me, Meg and Laurie tonight? His grandfather has these glamorous tickets for Covent Garden – it'll be amazing.

Beth   I've got to fix the chicken coop.

Jo   Leave that for once.

Amy   I'll come.

Jo   You're grounded.

Amy   Please! I'm sorry about the stupid jacket.

Jo   Forget it, little sister.

Amy   You never give me a chance.

Jo   You get first chances, second chances, third chances, and you still don't learn.

Amy   You're so mean. My future is at stake right now. Shouldn't my own sister show a bit of love in my hour of need?

Jo   Oh Amy! What do you know about need?

Jo *goes.* **Amy** *tries to put her portfolio back together.*

Beth   It doesn't matter what you wear, Amy. They'll love you and your drawings.

Amy   She messed everything up.

Beth   She loses her rag, it's just Jo. Maybe you're a bit alike…

Amy   You are joking!

Beth   I only mean you both feel passionately about things.

Amy   She thinks I've got to learn a lesson – what about her?

Beth   Let me do that – you get ready.

Amy *exits.* **Beth** *tidies the portfolio.* **Amy** *returns, perhaps with the suggestion of something in her bag.*

Beth   Are you ok?

Amy   Fine.

Beth   Just let it go, Amy. You'll be amazing.

(*Transition music: 'Atlantic' by Sleeping at Last.*)

Act 1, Scene 8

The March family sitting room: **Amy**, **Meg**, **Beth** *and* **Jo**. **Amy** *is studiously ignoring everyone, apparently reading.*

Meg   The curtain rises. The lights come up. We're on a deserted stage, it's the middle of baking Spain.

Jo   Meg loved it, can you tell?

Meg   The women from the cigar factory are sleeping.

Beth   Was Laurie's scary grandfather there?

Jo   And his dull tutor...

Meg   He wasn't dull.

Jo   (*impression of Brooke*) 'Sorry, may I squeeze by – apologies, I seem to have dropped something – oh dear, did I tread on your bag?'

Meg   He wasn't like that at all.

Jo   'After you, Meg! Can I get you an ice cream, Meg? You must let me lend you this book, Meg. Why don't you come along to the soup kitchen tomorrow, you'd love it, such a great vibe!'

Beth   Soup kitchen?

Meg   As well as working pretty hard as a teacher and being really good at it, Brooke finds the time to volunteer. Which is more than some people do.

Jo *exits, rolling her eyes about* **Brooke**.

Beth   Baking Spain.

Meg   Yes.

Beth   Don't worry about Jo. She's just a bit out of sorts.

Amy   Huh...

Beth   She's meeting Laurie later. He'll cheer her up.

Meg   Yes, well. All of a sudden—

Jo *returns.*

Jo   Where's my story?

Meg   Where did you leave it?

Jo   In the box in my room.

Beth   Perhaps you moved it.

Jo   Right before I left, I gathered everything up and put it in the box for safekeeping. I definitely left it right there – I would remember if I had done anything else.

Beth   I haven't seen it.

Jo   Amy?

Amy, *reading, ignores her.*

Jo   Amy, have you taken it?

Amy   What?

Jo   My story.

No answer. **Jo** *snatches the book* **Amy** *is reading.*

Jo   Give it back.

Amy   What?

Jo   You have, haven't you?

Amy   You always assume I'm in the wrong.

Jo   I can see right through you and out the other side. Give it back. Or I'll make you.

Amy   Can't.

Jo   Then I'll turn your room upside down—

Amy   You won't find it.

Jo   What do you mean?

Amy   You'll never see your stupid story again.

Jo   What have you done...

Amy   I burnt it. See how you like that.

Jo   You wouldn't, not even you.

Amy   Not *even* me?

Jo   That's my only copy.

Amy   Serves you right with your pretentious typewriter. You treat me like a little idiot—

Meg   Stop digging, Amy—

Jo   It's the only thing I've ever been proud of! I can never write it again.

Amy   Perhaps this will teach *you* a lesson.

Jo   Teach *me* a lesson!

Beth   Amy, say you're sorry.

Jo   She hasn't the capacity to be sorry for anything that isn't about her!

Jo *attacks* **Amy**.

Jo   You nasty little brat!

Amy   Meg, she's pulling my hair!

Jo   You've no idea of anyone outside yourself!

Amy   You should stop treating me like a child—

Jo   You spoilt, disgusting—

Amy   She's hurting me!

Jo   I hate you, Amy March!

Meg   Stop it – you'll kill her!

Jo   Good!

Ma *enters on a tableau of wrath and vengeance – which disassembles into silence when they see her.*

Ma   I'm waiting.

Amy   Jo treats me like a little kid and doesn't even care about leaving me out and making me feel small and not helping when I really, really need it. Doesn't she, Meg?

Meg   Don't look at me.

Amy   Beth – doesn't Jo care more about her stupid story than she does about her own sister?

Beth   She'd nearly finished it.

Ma   Jo?

Jo   She burnt my story. It's all gone. I can't ever get it back.

Amy   She provoked me!

Ma   You burnt Jo's story?

Amy   Yes.

Ma   What were you thinking?

Amy   I don't know...

Ma   How could a daughter of mine do something so nasty?

Amy   She wouldn't lend me her jacket...

Ma   Her jacket! For once I'm glad your father isn't here.

Amy   I'm sorry, Ma.

Amy *is upset.*

Ma   It's not me you owe an apology to, Amy.

Amy   I'm very, very sorry, Jo. I really am.

Jo   Sorry for what you did or sorry you've been found out?

(*Transition music: 'Algeria' by Sleeping at Last.*)

Act 1, Scene 9

Street outside the soup kitchen: **Meg** *and* **Brooke**, *dressed warmly.*

Brooke Sorry about all the washing up.

Meg Don't worry, I'm used to it.

Brooke What did you think?

Meg It's a lot more fun than I expected.

Brooke They loved you.

Meg *is quiet.*

Brooke You alright?

Meg Just a bit sad. I can't imagine not having a home.

Brooke Makes you value your good luck.

Meg Yeah. It's cold.

Brooke Here, have my scarf.

Brooke *wraps his scarf around* **Meg**.

Meg Thank you.

Brooke You're welcome.

Brooke *lingers just a moment more than he might. He checks himself quickly and moves away.*

Brooke Oh – I brought the book I mentioned – sorry if I went on about it the other night.

Brooke *hands* **Meg** *a book.*

Meg (*reading title, unsure*) *What Colour is your Parachute?*

Brooke Don't dismiss it – I know it looks like a trashy job-seeker's self-help manual – and that's because it is – but trashy self-help manuals can change your life. It says so on the back.

Meg And you're the living proof...

Brooke Found it in a charity shop. Never looked back.

Meg Right. So what did it teach you?

Brooke Stuff I didn't expect.

Meg Like what?

Brooke Like, I didn't want to work on my parents' farm.

Meg No – you grew up shovelling muck?

Brooke Real rural boy. Though we leave quite a lot of muck where it falls. It's good for the fields.

Meg How on earth did you end up teaching history?

Brooke Found out—

Meg —What colour your parachute was? Got it. Doesn't mean a thing to me.

Meg *returns the book.*

Brooke It's like – every little boy's dream is to drive a tractor. I have lived the dream. It was so boring.

Meg Whereas history...

Brooke Prussian Empire, Hundred Years War, Black Death – it all made sense!

Meg What did your parents think?

Brooke You can't live the wrong life just to please everyone else.

Meg   No. I suppose.

Brooke   The trick is to untangle what you want from everyone around you. Give it a try.

Meg   Now?

Brooke   Yup.

Meg   Oh. OK. Right. Jo wants me to do something ambitious, preferably something she'd like to do. Beth wants me to live at home forever more. Amy wants me to marry someone rich so she can be an artist living rent-free in my loft. Ma wants me to find my own path, which means she won't say.

Brooke   And what about you?

Meg   I don't know ... I'm sick of feeling replaceable. I want to feel needed, and knowledgeable, and skilled. I'd like to get to the end of each day and know that something practical and real changed because of me. If you can tell me which page that's on I ... What?

Brooke   Nothing.

Meg   I bet you never felt uncertain about anything – you went straight from trudging over the fields to first year under-graduate.

Brooke   Actually, pretty much. It's the way I am. I decide some-thing, I go for it. And if it doesn't work, nothing is lost.

Meg   I'll read the book.

She takes it.

Brooke   Might you come again next week?

Meg   I definitely might.

There's a moment when there might almost be a kiss.

Meg   OK bye then!

Meg *dashes off still wearing the scarf.*

(*Transition music: 'Enabling Environment' by Sleeping at Last.*)

Act 1, Scene 10

Hampstead Pond: **Jo**, *muffled up warm, stares out over the ice.* **Laurie** *creeps up and surprises her.*

Jo   Laurie!

Laurie What's up?

Jo   Nothing.

Laurie Did you row with Amy?

Jo   Don't ask.

Laurie Only she told me there'd been words.

Jo   Did she.

Laurie Think she wants to make up.

Jo *doesn't reply.*

Laurie She made me tell her we were going to the park—

Jo   Let's have a race!

Laurie You're on! Where?

Jo   Across the ice?

Laurie What? Jo. No.

Jo   Why not?

Laurie This isn't Canada, your quaint English ice is only an inch thick.

Jo   I'm going to try it.

Jo takes a step onto the frozen ice.

Laurie What's got into you?

Jo takes another step, deliberately winding him up.

Jo   See...

Laurie Don't go into the middle.

Jo   Stop worrying.

Jo takes another step. **Laurie** *goes while calling back to her.*

Laurie I'm going to get a stick in case you fall in – I'll see if there's a shrink around while I'm at it.

Jo   I'm fine!

Jo takes another step – there is a slight cracking sound. She looks up and sees **Amy** *appear on the opposite side of the pond.*

Amy   *(calling)* Jo, wait for me, I'm coming – please wait!

Jo watches her but says nothing. **Amy** *runs onto the ice – we hear a giant crack.*

Amy   Jo!

Blackout.

(Transition music: 'One in Ten' by Sleeping at Last.)

Act 1, Scene 11

The March family home. **Ma** *is dabbing TCP on* **Jo**'s *hand.*

Ma   Does it hurt?

Jo *winces but shakes her head.*

Ma   It looks sore.

Jo   It's nothing.

Ma   It's a nasty cut. Thank goodness you were there. If it hadn't been for you—

Jo   Laurie pulled her out.

Ma   You helped. You've had an awful shock. When I think what might have happened – you might have fallen through yourself—

Jo   I wish I had.

Ma   Don't be so hard on yourself.

Jo   Ma, I heard the ice cracking and I didn't warn her.

Ma   You didn't have time—

Jo   I did. I wanted something terrible to happen to her for once.

Ma   Jo...

Jo   If she'd got trapped under the ice it would have been my fault. I wish I had fallen in. I wish both my hands were cut to ribbons.

Jo *is upset.*

Ma Right, Jo March. Dry your face. You're going to promise me you'll remember this day so there'll never be another like it.

Jo How can I promise that – look what I did! I'm horrible. When I get angry, I lose sight of everything. It's like being possessed.

Ma We all have our bosom enemies Jo – don't make excuses.

Jo You don't understand because you never lose your temper.

Ma And was I born that way?

Jo Yes...?

Ma Rubbish. I work at it. And if I can, you can.

Jo I don't know how.

Ma Not good enough. Listen. When your father realised he wasn't going to get better, we talked about what would happen when he was gone. Those were hard conversations, Jo.

Jo I didn't mean to—

Ma Be quiet and listen. I have stuck to those plans no matter what. When my compass seems lost I have Michael in my mind. When anger rises over something stupid or petty, I remember him and I stop it. When I read the trust you girls have for me in your faces, I know all that effort was worth it. Don't tell me I don't have a temper. I lost a husband and raised four daughters alone. I could have screamed and shouted every single day. But I didn't. And I don't. And I won't. So, learn, and promise me you won't ever let it control you again.

Jo Sorry, Ma.

Ma Pardon?

Jo   I promise.

Ma   Right. Get yourself to bed. Start again tomorrow. Now, I'm going to see if Amy's ever getting out of that bath.

Ma *goes.* **Jo** *flings herself onto the sofa feeling terrible.* **Meg** *comes in aglow, still wearing the scarf.*

Meg   Evening!

Jo   Whose is that?

Meg   Brooke's. I'm in the mood for a midnight snack – is there anything to eat? Jo?

Jo   I don't know. I thought you went to a soup kitchen. Wasn't there soup?

Meg   Do you have to be sarcastic?

Meg *is singing to herself – perhaps a theme from Carmen.*

Jo   Are you drunk?

Meg   Nope.

Jo   What then?

Meg   If I tell you will you promise not to judge?

Jo   Yes.

Meg   I think I might, maybe, a tiny bit … like Brooke.

Jo *scoffs.*

Meg   What? He's actually really interesting, he grew up on a farm—

Jo *sniggers again.*

Meg   And he's kind of, quiet, and thoughtful. Plus, he's got lovely eyes when he smiles.

Jo   You sound like a Jane Austen heroine – 'So he has five thousand a year, but is he kind?'

Meg   You don't have to be like that, Jo.

Jo   Don't listen to me – be a farmer's wife if you want.

Meg   Why do you always have to burst everyone's bubble? You can't just let me be happy.

Act 1, Scene 12

The March family living room. **Beth** *is fixing a musical box for Ruby while* **Amy** *tries to draw her.*

Amy   Beth keep still.

Beth   Something's stuck...

Meg *enters, ready to go out.*

Meg   Scarf or no scarf?

Amy   Can't you find one that's not brown?

Meg   Why don't I own anything nice?

Amy   Beth how can I get your face if you keep moving?

Jo *enters with her typewriter and scarlet writing hat.*

Jo   The radiator's not working – I'm going to have to work in here.

Amy   Great, genius burns...

Jo   It's my living room too.

Jo *knocks into* **Beth**, *who catches her hand with the screwdriver.*

Beth   Ow!

Meg   Careful, Mouse.

Amy   That was totally Jo's fault.

Jo   It was an accident – are you OK?

Meg   (*tending to* **Beth**) Perfect. I'm already running late.

Beth   It's really bleeding.

Meg   Have I run out of plasters...?

Meg *fishes out a plaster from her bag as* **Jo** *puts on her writing hat and starts bashing away on the typewriter.*

Amy   Do you have to do that in here? My head hurts enough already.

Jo   Just like to do my writing where I can keep an eye on it.

Beth   It is quite noisy, Jo... but the bedroom is cold.

Jo *batters away with renewed ferocity.*

Beth   Ouch.

Meg   Should you be doing that at all if you don't know how to do it safely?

Jo   That is such a Meggish comment.

Beth   I don't know how else to fix it.

Amy   Then don't. Ruby won't know.

Beth   I'll know.

Jo   Beth doesn't like other people suffering.

Beth   It stings...

Amy (*shouting over the typewriter*) Well it's your fault.

Ma *enters, unseen.*

Beth It was an accident.

Meg I've got to go.

Jo Where to?

Amy (*teasing*) She's meeting Brooke.

Meg Shut up Amy.

Jo (*sarcastic*) Have fun!

Meg I will!

Beth You all don't need to shout.

Amy Seems like I do!

Jo Will you shut up!

Amy Will you shut up!

Ma What on earth is going on here?

The sisters ad lib all at the same time about who they are annoyed at and why.

Ma Stop! Now! As if it isn't hard enough dealing with scared mothers and bad-tempered doctors all day I come home and find my living room full of squabbling babies. What on earth have I been doing all these years? I obviously wasn't teaching you how to behave. At least when you were actual toddlers you were sweet.

Jo Ma, we really—

Ma I don't want to hear it! I'm going to bed. I haven't got a bone that isn't aching. If I don't lie down soon my body may overrule my mind. Maybe when I wake up, this won't have happened. Maybe, if I sleep really deeply, I'll dream I've got four nearly adult daughters I can be proud of. Goodnight.

Mutterings of goodnight as **Ma** *goes.*

Loaded pause. **Jo** *spies the Northern Lights voucher still lying on* **Ma***'s desk.*

Jo   The voucher...

Meg   What?

Jo   For Christmas, her present – she never rang up.

Meg   She probably thinks we couldn't manage without her.

Beth   Look at us. She's right.

Jo   It's too late for the Northern Lights.

Meg   We could find something else—

Amy   We could ask Hannah at work to go with her.

Beth   I hate that we made her upset.

Meg   We're going to put it right, Mouse. Right?

(*Transition music: 'Just Listen' by Sleeping at Last.*)

Act 1, Scene 13

The March family living room. **Ma** *and the girls are gathered amid much excitement.* **Ma** *has her suitcase packed.*

Meg   Cab's waiting.

Ma   I'm not ready...

Jo   You've got your passport and tickets – what else matters?

Ma   Sun cream!

Amy   In the side pocket.

Beth   Here's your suitcase.

Ma   I've put my handbag down...

Jo   Got it.

Ma   Jo – good luck at university.

Jo   Thanks Ma.

Ma   I can't believe I won't be here for your first day.

Amy   She's not five, Ma!

Jo   You'll be having too much fun to even think about it.

Amy   You'll be lying on the beach next to Hannah watching the sun set.

Ma   I can't quite believe this is happening.

Meg   Ma, you should really go.

Ma   I forgot – housekeeping.

Meg   I'll sort it – it's only a couple of weeks.

Ma   I've put some cash in the tin – you'll need to budget.

Jo   We can manage...

Ma   Divide it up for each week and leave a bit over for emergencies.

Meg   Yes Ma.

Ma   Check with Meg before you spend any. Share out the chores. Be nice to each other.

Jo   We promise.

Amy   I nearly forgot—

Amy *hands over a parcel.*

Ma   Don't think I can take any more presents.

Amy   You'll need this one.

Ma *opens it. Inside is a one-piece swimsuit.*

Ma   Oh my God. Imagine me!

Beth   Have a fantastic time, Ma.

Ma *is moved.*

Jo   It's just a swimming costume.

Ma   I can't remember the last time I was away from you girls for more than a few hours.

Amy   We're practically grown-ups.

Meg   I'll look after them.

Ma *steels herself.*

Ma   Oh my handbag—

Jo   You've got it!

Ma   Right. Right.

She hugs each girl in turn.

Ma   Right.

She takes up her suitcase, she pulls herself together.

Ma   Bye bye, darlings.

Ma *goes.*

(Transition music: 'You are Enough' by Sleeping at Last.)

Act 1, Scene 14

Summer at the park. Each of the four sisters is kitted out in her own manner for an encounter with the sunny outdoors. **Meg** *has the book that Brooke gave her,* **Jo** *reads poetry,* **Beth** *is making a box,* **Amy** *is sketching. They settle to their activities with a dedicated air – though* **Meg** *keeps breaking off to stare into the distance.*

Jo   So, have you identified your parachute colour yet, Meg?

Meg   Making progress, thanks Jo. How's the poetry?

Jo   Uplifting.

Beth   Is that Laurie by the pond?

Amy   Ignore him – he'll distract us.

Jo   It's a public park.

Beth   He's seen us.

Beth *waves.*

Amy   Don't move – you'll spoil my picture.

Jo   Right, test me, Beth.

Jo *hands* **Beth** *her book.*

Jo   (*reciting from memory*) 'The silver swan who living had no note, when death approached unlocked her silver throat—'

Beth   Silent.

Jo   'Silent throat. Leaning her breast into the reedy shore, she sang her first and last and sang no more—'

Amy   Can't you learn something more cheerful?

Meg   Do swans really sing as they die?

Jo   I thought you were concentrating.

Laurie *enters.*

Laurie   Hi ladies. I hope I'm not bothering you.

Amy   Well actually—

Jo   Of course not.

Laurie   I was just having a wander. Passing the fretful hour. Time to burn.

Amy   (*uninterested*) Aha.

Laurie   But I can head off if it's inconvenient. I can see you're all really busy. Not that I need company as I await my results – congrats by the way, Amy, got what you needed for sixth form.

Amy   (*offhand*) Thanks.

Jo   Oh for goodness sake let him sit down.

Amy   We said—

Jo But it's only Laurie!

Beth Do you really get your results today?

Laurie Yup. The day of doom. But don't worry. This poor lonely boy doesn't really need the comfort of your company. I'll be ok...

Amy Fine. If he obeys the rules.

Laurie *joins them.*

Laurie You know me – 'only Laurie' – I love rules! Lay them on me.

Amy We are improving ourselves.

Laurie Damn – that's me out. I'm perfect already.

Amy We're not lying around being idle like some people, who only end up bored and annoying and getting under other people's feet—

Laurie She's badmouthing you again, Beth...

Amy Perfection of the self is the highest form of art.

Meg God, Amy!

Laurie What are you perfecting, Beth?

Beth A music box for baby Ruby.

Laurie Under these strict rules, am I allowed to read?

Laurie *pulls out a women's magazine.*

Meg Women's Weekly?

Laurie Publishes some pretty innovative stuff actually. Listen to this one – 'The Rival Painter', a short story by—

Jo Give me that—

Laurie *keeps it out of* **Jo***'s reach.*

Meg Jo? Don't tell me—

Beth Did they publish your story?

Laurie 'By Jo March.'

Beth That's brilliant!

Amy How much did you get for it?

Jo They don't pay on spec, but they said they might commission me if their readers like it.

Beth I always knew you'd do something amazing.

Jo It's just a silly romance – I wanted to see if I could do it. The next thing I write is going to be much better.

Laurie It was good enough to print. You got the key to your castle, Miss Authoress.

Jo Some old trash in a magazine hardly counts—

Beth Laurie, Brooke's coming.

Amy Look at his face.

Laurie Get your black cap on, Jo.

Jo Is there nowhere he doesn't take the sensible umbrella...?

Brooke *enters with an umbrella and an envelope.*

Brooke Courage, mon brave.

Brooke *gives Laurie the envelope.*

Laurie Here's my doom. Can somebody?

Laurie *tries to give the envelope to* **Jo***.*

Jo   It's your future. You open it.

Amy   Oh for goodness' sake.

Amy *takes the envelope and takes out a piece of paper.*

Laurie   So? Berlin jazz bar or Edinburgh school of bore? Not that I want to make it sound like one of those is better than the other.

Amy   Gosh Laurie.

They pass the paper around.

Meg   Well done, Brooke...

Jo   Amazing...

Beth   You did it!

Laurie   (*flatly*) I did it.

Meg   Your grandfather will be thrilled.

Laurie   Won't he though.

Amy   I wish I could go away.

Jo   What are you going to do now, Brooke?

Brooke I've got a new job, assistant head of department.

Laurie   Nice work, Brooke.

Meg   So you're staying?

Brooke Looks like it.

Laurie   I taught him everything he knows.

Beth   Let's celebrate – Laurie's exams, Jo's story—

Amy   Me liberated from school—

Meg Getting Ma to go on holiday!

Laurie Brooke being freed from tutoring me!

Something falls on **Meg**.

Meg Is that rain?

Jo You're kidding...

Brooke Summer storm – it *was* forecast. Actually, I'm supposed to be at the soup kitchen. Meg are you...?

Meg Yeah, definitely.

Laurie I should really go and see grandfather. Have a very sober two-man party.

Jo Make it three – I'll see if I can un-sober things a bit.

Amy I need to finish these drawings.

Beth (*disappointed*) Oh.

Meg We'll celebrate another night.

The rain is really setting in – they rush to gather up their stuff.

Amy My picture!

Meg (*to* **Brooke**) Thank God you brought an umbrella!

Laurie (*to* **Jo**) Come on Miss Authoress.

Jo See you at home, Mouse.

They scatter, **Meg** *and* **Brooke** *one way,* **Laurie** *and* **Jo** *another,* **Amy** *heading off on her own mission.* **Beth** *goes last, removing her jacket to protect the precious music box for Ruby.*

(Transition music: 'Atlantic' by Sleeping at Last.)

Act 1, Scene 15

The March family sitting room. **Meg** *has the housekeeping tin.* **Jo** *has a book.* **Amy** *enters.*

Amy   How do you spell 'sepulchre'?

Jo   I don't.

Meg   If you're writing to Ma then that isn't the kind of thing she needs.

Amy   I'm naming an artwork.

Jo   Where's Beth?

Amy   Visiting baby Ruby.

Meg   Did you let her do all that washing up?

Amy   She offered.

Jo   It was your turn!

Amy   Meg said she'd find someone to fix the dishwasher.

Jo   That's not the point

Meg *holds up the housekeeping tin.*

Meg   (*to* **Amy**) Do you know where that twenty from the housekeeping went?

Jo   There's absolutely nothing in the cupboards so it can't have gone on food...

Amy   I needed clay and paints.

Meg   Amy!

Amy   How am I supposed to get on without materials?

Meg   Ma said ask first! Hope it's worth it because you're on lentils now.

Beth *enters, in shock.*

Jo   Beth? What's the matter?

Beth   Ruby's dead.

Jo   What?

Beth   She had a cold...

Meg   Sit down, Mouse.

Beth   She was just snuffly and hot but then her breathing got really fast and kind of fluttery. I called an ambulance, her Mum was screaming. She was lying in my arms, then she gave this awful sigh and trembled and went still. Her lips were blue. I tried to do the kiss of life how Ma showed us but nothing happened.

Meg   Oh Beth...

Jo   How is that possible?

Beth   The paramedic said it might have been pneumonia.

Amy   They can treat pneumonia!

Beth   She was so little. It was so fast—

Meg   You've had a shock – Amy get her some water.

Jo   Beth are you ok?

Meg   Of course she's not.

Jo   No, I mean – really ok.

Meg *puts her hand to* **Beth**'*s forehead.*

Beth   I feel alright.

Meg   I don't think you are.

Jo   We should call Ma.

Meg   It's just a temperature.

Jo   That she got from a really sick baby.

Amy   We should definitely call Ma.

Meg   Would you two calm down? Don't listen to them Beth, you're going to be fine. You've got a touch of something. You've had a shock. Amy where's that water? I'm going to get you some paracetamol.

Beth   Thank you, Meg.

Jo   (*to* **Meg**) Paracetamol?

Meg   We can handle this, we're not children.

Jo   Shouldn't we get her to a doctor first?

Amy   Jo's right.

Meg   What is this?

Beth   Oh dear...

Jo   It's not about you Meg—

Meg   What are you talking about?

Amy   What is it Beth?

Beth   I think I'm maybe going to...

Beth *faints.* (*Transition music: 'Indian' by Sleeping at Last.*)

Act 1, Scene 16

Hospital: night. **Beth** *is unconscious in a hospital bed,* **Meg** *and* **Jo** *watch over her.* **Amy** *is sleeping.*

Jo   Meg. Do antibiotics ever... not work?

Meg   No.

Jo   That's not true is it?

Meg   No.

Jo   Meg, please can we—

Meg   No – look, in a bit we'll ask the doctor again and in the morning we'll decide whether to call Ma or not. Promise.

Jo   I just really want her.

Meg   Then that's about you, isn't it?

Jo   It's about Beth—

Meg   Sorry. Come here.

Meg *hugs* **Jo.**

Meg   Beth is going to be OK. She's where she needs to be.

Jo   Do you remember Dad in hospital?

Meg   Yes.

Pause.

Meg   Do you ever speak to him? Dad?

Jo   No. You?

Meg *shakes her head.*

Pause.

Meg   Ma does.

Jo   Does she? What does she talk about?

Meg   Us.

Laurie *enters.*

Laurie   Only me.

Meg   Laurie?

Jo   How did you know?

Laurie   Sort of chain of concern. Grandfather spotted the ambulance.

Meg   Will you stay with Jo while I see the duty doctor?

Laurie   Sure.

Meg   (*aside to* **Laurie**, *indicating* **Jo**) Help me out...

Meg *goes.*

Jo   I'm glad to see you.

Laurie   That bad is it? How's the patient?

Jo   Awful.

Laurie   And Beth?

Jo   That's not funny. Look at her. It's like she's made out of marble. Everyone keeps telling us we have to wait.

Laurie   Can I get you anything? Sandwich? Cup of your English tea?

Jo   You know what I really want?

Laurie   A big old hug?

Jo   I want Ma.

Laurie Oh.

Jo Meg's being super protective but if something happens to Beth and Ma's not here—

Laurie Actually, about your Ma...

Jo What?

Laurie You know what grandfather's like – busybody, thinks he knows best how to conduct everyone else's life, that sort of thing... Anyway, he told your Ma.

Jo Is she coming?

Laurie He roped me in to pick her up from the airport.

Jo Oh Laurie!

Jo *flings herself into* **Laurie**'s *arms.*

Laurie Wow!

Jo How was she?

Laurie He didn't say, just passed on the message that I was to check on you. Which I, like a knight errant, swore to do.

Jo Thanks.

Laurie Hey, fling yourself into my arms again.

Jo Get out of here and get my Ma.

Meg *enters.*

Jo What did he say?

Meg He said, wait. But maybe tell Ma, in case of complications.

Jo What complications?

Meg   He's just being extra cautious. Sometimes other viruses can get in and damage the heart and stuff—

Jo   The heart?

Meg   Only sometimes. Doesn't mean it's happened. I'm sure she's going to be fine.

Laurie   Your Ma's on her way – blame grandfather. Oh – guess what else, Brooke's downstairs. Shall I send him up?

Meg *is uncertain.*

Meg   No thank you.

Laurie   You sure? I can just…

Meg   Not now. Not at this moment.

Laurie   What should I tell him?

Meg   Just tell him I don't want to see him! Just. One thing at a time. Please.

Laurie   (*trying to lighten the mood*) Aye aye captain. (*To* **Jo**) Look after my best girl.

Laurie *goes. Pause.*

Jo   Is there nowhere he won't—

Meg   Don't say anything Jo. Please.

Pause.

Jo   I don't know what I'd do without you.

(Transition music: 'Her Joy Was Complete' by Sleeping at Last.)

Act 1, Scene 17

Hospital: dawn. **Meg**, **Jo**, **Amy** *are asleep by* **Beth***'s bed.* **Ma** *enters. She goes to* **Beth**, *who opens her eyes.*

Beth   You're back.

Ma   The tricks you girls will pull to get my attention.

Beth   Baby Ruby died.

Ma   I know darling. I'm so sorry.

Beth   Have you spoken to the doctor?

Ma   Yes.

Beth   Am I going to be alright?

Ma *steels herself to shield Beth.*

Ma   Absolutely.

Beth   I feel tired.

Ma   Have a little snooze.

Ma *helps* **Beth** *settle herself.* **Beth** *closes her eyes.*

Ma   My poor baby...

Jo *wakes – she jumps up, disturbing* **Meg** *and* **Amy**.

Jo   You're here!

Amy   Ow!

Meg   It's Ma.

Ma   You'll wake up Beth.

Jo   Nothing wakes her.

Ma   Not true. I've just had a lovely chat.

Jo   Did she speak?

Ma   She did.

Meg   Have you seen the doctor?

Ma   Yes. She's much better, look at her.

Jo   What about complications?

Ma   (*to* **Amy**) When did you last sleep in a bed?

Amy   We missed you.

Ma   I tell you what, why don't I get us breakfast in the canteen – I bet you haven't eaten a thing.

Jo   (*watching over* **Beth**) Is she really better?

Ma   Absolutely. Absolutely.

(Transition music: 'Laurie Winter Song' by Ingrid Michaelson & Sara Bareilles.)

Act 1, Scene 18

The March family living room: Christmas Eve. **Jo** *is wrapping a present for Aunt March while* **Meg** *and* **Amy** *prepare the house,* **Laurie** *twangles a guitar and* **Beth** *unscrews bulbs from the fairy lights to see which one is the loose connection.*

Meg   Are those lights ready?

The lights flash on and off.

Beth   Nope.

Jo   How come we put them away working every year and when we get them out they're broken again? (*To* **Laurie**) Can you help?

Laurie   Isn't soothing your soul enough?

Jo   If it did.

Laurie   I tell you whose soul could do with soothing.

Jo   Who?

Laurie   Brooke's. He seems to have picked up some kind of illness. Keeps giving these deep long sighs... Meg, maybe you should look in on him. Take his temperature – it'd be good practice now you're all set on being a nurse.

Meg   I'm cooking.

Laurie   Oh, fine. You'd have to be quick anyway – says he's giving up his job and going back to the farm. Poor old Brooke.

Amy   That's a prospect to depress anyone.

Jo   Aunt March is done.

Jo *holds out a scruffily wrapped present.*

Amy What have you done to that?

Jo It was an awkward shape.

Amy It's a tin of shortbread.

Beth *throws down the lights.*

Jo What's up, Mouse?

Beth Nothing.

Meg (*to* **Jo**) Ruby would have been one today.

Jo Oh Beth…

Beth I made her mum a little box for keepsakes. I thought I'd take it over before dinner, if there's time.

Amy I'll come. (*She holds up Aunt March's present.*) We can drop this off at the same time.

Meg Don't be too long.

Amy *and* **Beth** *go to the door –* **Brooke** *is hovering outside.*

Amy Brooke.

Brooke Hi! Just… popping over.

Amy Yeah bye.

Amy *and* **Beth** *go.*

Brooke Meg! So good to see you. I just…

Brooke *notices* **Laurie** *and* **Jo**.

Brooke Oh…

Laurie Hey Brooke – how's things?

Brooke Good.

Awkward pause.

Brooke Did I leave my umbrella? I think I left my umbrella. Have you seen it Jo?

Jo No.

Brooke Oh. You sure? Not lying around... somewhere else?

Jo *ignores him.* **Meg** *and* **Brooke** *stare at each other.* **Laurie** *sees that they want to be alone and tries to distract* **Jo**.

Brooke Just a thought. (*To* **Meg**) I'm going away.

Jo Yes, Laurie told us.

Meg I'm sorry things haven't worked out. How've you been?

Brooke Good. And Beth?

Meg Better.

Brooke Happy to hear it.

Laurie Can you smell burning?

Meg Jo could you...

Jo It's your sauce.

Meg Please Jo.

Laurie Brooke can help – he's a dab hand in the kitchen.

Meg *and* **Brooke** *go.*

Laurie Mr and Mrs Right...

Jo Oh please!

The lights flash again.

Laurie   Alright then – Mrs Right and Mr Persistent.

Jo   He wants the whole domestic blister.

Laurie   He's a nice man.

Jo   Nice! If Meg ends up with Brooke she'll disappear under a pile of neatly ironed washing and a stack of nappies before you can say 'housewife'. And then who will I have?

Laurie   You've got me there... Can't stop people falling in love.

Jo   It's not love, it's a mental disorder.

Laurie   It'll happen to you.

Jo   Sentimentality makes me heave.

Laurie   Don't tell me there's no one at uni?

Jo   Uni is dull professors dissecting books. There lies literature – dead on the surgeon's table. I might as well be studying biology – no, something more gruesome. Forensics. Cutting up dead people – cutting up the creative soul, slashing its veins, draining the life blood—

Laurie   You'll fall for some poet, then we'll be left pining.

Jo   You're the only one breaking hearts. Who's the latest in Edinburgh?

Laurie   In Edinburgh, no one.

Jo   You fall in love, like, once a week.

Laurie   In love, no. I've got this problem I can't shift.

Jo   They'll have a cream for that.

Laurie   It's a more chronic condition. It's got a strange name – it's called Josephine.

Jo   Oh.

Laurie Yes. Maybe you can help.

Jo   I'm not such an agony aunt...

Laurie Good, because I'm trying to avoid agony, though it's not going so well. Thing is, I love you. I love only you. I've always loved you. I've tried curing it in the traditional manner but nobody else works. So I can't do anything about it, except, tell you.

Jo   Oh. Crap.

Laurie It is for me. How is it for you?

Jo   I'm really sorry, Laurie.

Laurie That sounds bad.

Jo   I love you as a friend.

Laurie That's really not the same thing.

Jo   You'll find someone much better. You deserve someone who's head over heels with you.

Laurie I sure do. Can't change this though.

Jo   I'm sorry.

Laurie You care more about your scribbling than you do about me.

Jo   I don't. Just, I can't get on without it.

Laurie But you can without me.

Jo   I feel like I've stabbed you.

Laurie It would save me a job.

Jo   I'm so, so sorry Laurie.

Laurie Anything more? Then I'll just be off to Westminster Bridge.

Jo   Don't joke, Laurie, that's horrible.

Laurie Who said I'm joking.

Jo   Don't be like that.

Laurie Like what? You've washed your hands. Happy Christmas, Jo.

Laurie *goes.*

Music plays ('Algeria' by Sleeping at Last) as **Jo** *goes to the lights and starts aggressively trying to fix them. It's hopeless – she gives up and storms away. Behind her the lights flash on – she turns and sees* **Meg** *and* **Brooke** *kissing.*

Everything is about to change.

Blackout. Interval.

Act 2, Scene 1

The March family living room. Three years have passed. As the audience returns, music is playing ('Aperture' by Sleeping at Last). **Beth** *and* **Jo** *are mucking around on the sofa with the contents of the dressing-up box (perhaps the Santa hat is still in there somewhere) – two sisters having fun together, celebrating.* **Jo** *teams different crazy hats with a strange dress she has dug out. Once the audience is settled, music fades.*

Ma *enters.*

Ma   What have I told you about that sofa?

Jo   Ma – I've done it – I'm going to be a published author!

Jo *hands* **Ma** *a letter, which she reads.*

Ma   They accepted your book?

Jo   Don't sound so surprised.

Ma   I'm not – well done. Good God.

Jo   Beth, get Meg on the phone.

Ma   Wait a second...

Beth   What? What's wrong?

Ma   Have you actually read this through?

Jo *takes it.*

Jo   (*reading*) 'Dear Jo, it is with pleasure...' dah-da-dah! ... 'Cut by two thirds' ... 'remove description' – those are the best bits! – 'take out the preaching'!

Beth   There's isn't any preaching.

Jo   According to this it's jam-packed.

Beth   But if you do it they'll publish and you'll be a real author?

Jo   Of what though? Will it even be my book anymore?

Beth   You could write another.

Jo   And watch three more years just fly by, living at home, dependent on Ma.

Ma   I don't mind.

Jo   I mind. Three years. What do you think, Ma?

Ma   It's your baby, darling. All I can say is trust your instincts on this one.

Jo   Beth?

Beth   I just want to see your name on the cover of a book, Jo.

Jo *doesn't know what to do.*

Beth   Ma. I'm going for a lie down. (*Winking at* **Jo**) Too much excitement. (*To* **Ma**) Wake me in a bit?

Ma   OK, my darling.

Beth *goes.*

Jo   She's getting worse.

Ma   She's fine.

Ma *goes to her desk and begins writing up her clinical notes.* **Amy** *enters, dressed to impress and in a hurry.*

Amy   (*to* **Jo**) You're not seriously considering wearing that, are you?

Jo   (*sarcastic*) What? Don't you like it?

Amy   Don't joke around. What will Aunt March think?

Jo   What's she got to do with anything?

Amy   Jo – the garden party!

Amy *hunts for something to make* **Jo** *more presentable.*

Jo   Oh, I'm not going to that.

Amy   You promised!

Jo   I've done a great many rash and foolish things in my life, but agreeing to go to one of Aunt March's garden parties—

Amy   You did! And she especially asked me to bring you.

Jo   She didn't...

Amy   Well she asked me to bring 'Josephine'. Apparently, she has a favour to ask you.

Jo   Well you can tell her that 'Josephine' finds favours oppressive and they make her feel like a slave.

Amy   What is the harm in being nice to someone who could be nice to us back?

Jo   I don't know, what is the harm?

Amy   You know, that dress is kind of...

Jo   What?

Amy *removes* **Jo**'s *outlandish hat and gazes at her critically.*

Amy   Yeah. Interesting.

Jo   You go. I'll just say all the wrong things.

Amy   We won't stay long. Just stick to pleasantries. Honestly, it's a lot easier than you make out. All you have to do is be... normal. Please Jo, she's auctioning my painting for her charity thing...

Jo *looks over at* **Ma***, who signals amused encouragement.*

Jo   Argh! Alright.

Amy *goes and* **Jo** *follows – though unseen by* **Amy** *she jams the objectionable hat back on her head.* **Ma** *is alone on stage. She looks at her photo of Michael.*

Ma   Did you hear that, Michael? Jo's been working on that novel for three years, all through university. Cut it by two thirds. Ridiculous. (*Taking a deep breath*) Right, what else? Amy's art show – dear God! All these giant canvases on the wall by our baby girl, and then the last one, tiny, a little portrait she painted from your photograph. Knocked me for six. I was blinking so hard I'm sure her friends thought I had a medical condition. (*Pause*) We saw the heart specialist again. Thank God Beth works somewhere so understanding. I suppose reconditioning second hand furniture isn't exactly high pressure. If she's not feeling up to it, she just comes home. She comes home a lot. (*Pause.*) Oh, I took Meg a casserole. I know! Don't interfere, wait to be asked. Her nurse's uniform barely has the crease out of it and now look. But I keep telling her, your job will still be there the far side. I know, I've been there. Not that she can hear me. Poor lamb!

Act 2, Scene 2

Meg's home. **Meg** *enters with a baby monitor and sits wearily. She shuts her eyes.* **Jo** *enters.*

Jo   Hey mumma!

Meg   Argh...

Jo   It's your friendly local delivery service – nourishing soup and fresh bread.

Meg   Shh!

Meg *thinks she hears a whimper on the baby monitor.*

Meg   Sing a lullaby.

Jo   You know I can't sing.

Meg   Not me – two-way monitor. Brooke got it.

Jo   How is Brooke?

Jo *goes to do the impression.*

Meg   Not the impression, Jo...

Jo   Sorry. What does it do?

Meg   I hear them, they hear me.

Jo   Is that good?

Meg   It's supposed to soothe them.

Jo *hums tunelessly into the baby monitor.*

Meg   That'll give them nightmares.

Jo   Have you eaten?

Meg   I had some crackers.

Jo   Have you just basically been sitting here humming into a baby monitor and eating crackers?

Meg   No. I went to the loo.

Jo   Meg, are you getting any time to yourself?

Meg   You *are* joking.

Jo   I could babysit – you and Brooke could go for a walk.

Meg   When, Jo? They take an hour to feed – Daisy's a guzzler but Johnny keeps falling asleep – then another hour to wind and change, then they sleep for an hour tops *if* they decide to sleep at the same time, which isn't always – then it's time to feed again. So, yeah, not much time for myself.

Jo   Sorry, Meg. I just don't know about this stuff.

Meg   I'm not angry. I'm just really really really really tired.

Jo   What are the nights like?

Meg   Same. With the lights off. I basically haven't slept in five weeks.

Jo   How are you even alive?

Meg   I don't know. Am I?

Jo   Is Brooke helping?

Meg   I couldn't survive without him. He's taken over the cooking. He was already doing the washing.

Jo   That's good.

Meg   We've stopped cleaning for now.

Jo   How's his new job?

Meg   (*It's a new thought*) I don't know. I should know, shouldn't I... Right now, the country could be at war and I wouldn't have a clue. OK: I'm awake. Tell me everything that's happened that matters.

Jo   We're not at war. Currently. I signed off the proofs on my novel.

Meg   You finished it?

Jo   For better or worse.

Meg   For better, I'm certain.

Jo   It hurt, cutting it to ribbons.

Meg   But you did it.

Jo   Well just in case it doesn't make my fortune I've been applying for jobs ... teaching.

Meg   Teaching? Jo March?

Meg *hears a whimper on the monitor.*

Meg   Look, you scared my babies. Seriously?

Jo   I can't sit around doing zero at home forever.

Meg   Hey, don't knock sitting around at home.

Jo   You're not doing zero. There is nothing out there that's more important than what you're doing in here.

Meg   I miss work sometimes. I worry I'm going to forget everything.

Jo   One afternoon on the ward and it'll all come back. And meanwhile you've created two entire new human beings.

Meg   Do you know what's really mad? Sometimes when they're both asleep, I creep in and watch them. Sometimes an hour goes by. And I can't wait for them to open their eyes so I can see them again. Then they do and suddenly I've got these two crying babies in my arms, both hungry, and I've got to feed them and somehow change them both at the same time and I think – God, Meg, why didn't you sleep while you could!

Jo Sounds like love.

Meg Does, doesn't it.

Brooke *enters.*

Brooke Right, wash is on. I've managed to get most of the sick off the cushion and I've also ordered those breast... Oh, hi Jo.

Jo (*smiling*) Hi Brooke. How are you?

Brooke I've got no idea what time of day it is but other than that. Fine.

Meg (*to* **Brooke**) Thank you.

Jo I should go.

Jo *goes to leave, thinks better of it and suddenly bestows on* **Brooke** *a brief but sisterly hug. On her way out she stops and looks back at* **Meg** *and* **Brooke** *nestled together, now a family in their own right. (Transition music: 'Her Joy Was Complete' by Sleeping at Last.)*

Act 2, Scene 3

The March family living room. **Amy** *and* **Beth** *are reading reviews on the sofa.*

Beth This one's good – 'An exquisite book full of truth, beauty and earnestness'.

Amy She won't like earnestness. Uh-oh – 'Morbid fantasies, unnatural characters.'

Beth These critics! Listen – 'In places it is highly original, and there's no doubt it's written with great force and feeling, but overall the impression is one of muddle—'

Jo *enters. Silence.*

Jo I know. I've read them.

Beth Don't listen to them. They don't even agree.

Jo I just wish I'd printed it whole or not at all.

Amy Then you wouldn't have been published.

Ma *enters.*

Ma Ah. Hello girls.

Jo Did you see?

Ma Yup. Don't let them grind you down. If it doesn't ring true, ignore it.

Jo What about the bits that ring true and hurt?

Ma Those you may have to take on board.

Amy Did you see Aunt March?

Ma   Yes ... She was telling me about a little place she's bought in New York—

Amy   New York? I bet it's a mansion.

Ma   You may be right. She's looking for someone to house-sit for six months while it's done up.

Jo   Are you serious? Yes! Finally! At last working for her all those years pays off.

Ma   Sorry, Jo. She thought Amy might like to go.

Amy   Aunt March I love you!

Jo   What?

Ma   She'll pay you an allowance. Also, fees if you want to do some courses at the New York College of Art.

Amy   My future is beginning...

Ma   I did suggest you might both go. It seems Aunt March didn't think you'd make a very suitable house sitter.

Jo   Yes, well, sitting in a house probably takes more skill than you'd think.

Beth   You'd have to be nice to Aunt March – imagine when she came to stay...

Amy   (*alarmed*) Will she come to stay?

Ma   Don't think she plans to.

Jo   It's always the same – Amy has all the fun.

Amy   I earned this!

Ma   She did say she would have asked you, but you told her you hate people doing you favours.

Jo   I am such an idiot.

Amy   When does she want me to go?

Ma   As soon as you can.

Amy   I'm packing – wait till I tell everyone!

Amy *goes.*

Ma   Try not to spoil it for her.

Jo   She always gets what she wants and I never do.

Beth   I know it's selfish, Jo, but I'm glad you're not going away to New York.

Ma   Maybe one of those jobs will come up.

Pause.

Jo   Beth, how about we wash my ill-gotten earnings clean by taking you away somewhere wild and beautiful – a Scottish island!

Beth   I don't know...

Ma   Isn't that a bit remote?

Jo   It would do you good. Cornwall then – I don't care – Margate!

Beth   Margate...

Jo   It would be a favour to me – I need the breeze through my soul and some good sisterly company. Please.

Beth   Alright, let's go.

Jo   Now I don't care about novels, reviews or all the bright lights of Manhattan.

Jo *hugs* **Beth** *and whirls her round.*

Ma   Gently!

Jo   She's stronger than you think.

Ma   Beth?

Beth   I'll be fine. I'll be with Jo.

(*Transition music: 'Going Home' by Intrinsic Focus.*)

Act 2, Scene 4

By the sea: **Jo** *and* **Beth**.

Jo   OK. Marks out of ten.

Beth   Seeing the horizon, eleven. Temperature, three.

Jo   Cuddle up – you need to eat more.

Beth   Jo...

Jo   Shall we get some food?

Beth   I'm not hungry.

Jo   Your chickens eat more than you do. (*She pulls a blanket round* **Beth**) Is that better?

Beth   Much better.

Jo   Liar, you're freezing.

Beth   Jo, I need to tell you something.

Jo   Snap.

Beth   What?

Jo   I've got some news. You first.

Act 2

Beth   No. You go first.

Jo   Alright. What do you think? I've been offered a job!

Beth   A proper job?

Jo   I know. I saw this advert for a creative writing teacher.

Beth   And...

Jo   Well, it's this amazing international college. The students come from all over the world. I told them honestly about my book, that I really like to write, and that's what I'll be doing when I'm not teaching. And they said, when can you start?

Beth *is thrilled.*

Jo   I said I'd give them a yes or a no today.

Beth   You deserve this.

Jo   It's in Berlin.

Beth   Oh.

Jo   Now you're sad.

Beth   I'm not. You're going to make a fabulous teacher.

Jo   Not if I say no.

Beth   I won't let you do that.

Jo   But it'll be like leaving you behind. I need to know what you really, really think.

Beth   I think you should do it, and write down all the things you see and the people you meet and put them into stories and send them to me. Because I will love that.

Jo   You sure?

Beth   This is brilliant, Jo.

Jo   I haven't screwed it up yet – give me a chance.

Beth   You won't. You're going to be fantastic.

Jo   Your turn.

Beth   My turn what?

Jo   Your news.

Beth   (*making it up*) Meg rang – she said Daisy slept for five hours straight.

Jo   Are you alright?

Beth   I'm fine.

Jo   I can tell you're not.

Beth   Only, all your lives are rushing forward...

Jo   Your life can rush forward too. We could live together, Beth. I could save up in Berlin and then we could get our own place and you could make beautiful things and I could write and we could go into business!

Beth   (*laughing*) That's not a business, Jo.

Jo   I don't care! Where would you be if you could be anywhere, just you and me? You're not allowed to say home.

Beth   Here's pretty great.

Jo   By the sea?

Beth   By the sea.

(*Transition music: 'Atlantic' by Sleeping at Last.*)

Act 2, Scene 5

Meg *is on the sofa reading a postcard from* **Amy** *in New York.*

Amy   New York, Meg, I am in love! And Aunt's little place? Enormous. When I gave my address at college enrolment you could see everyone looking at me... Also, my accent. All I have to do to make everyone swoon is just open my mouth! Hey, do you remember a guy called Fred Vaughn? Said he'd met you – some friend of Sally's brother? He's over here working at a law firm. Sends me roses every day – I'm running out of buckets! You'll never guess what though – I'm having my own exhibition. I took two whole days getting the paintings hung perfectly in this fancy gallery so the evening light sets off the canvases just as everyone arrives on the dot of seven pm – dealers, critics, buyers. What else? Oh yeah, you know Laurie's in town. His grandfather sent him over to 'look into job opportunities' – as if. He spends half his time partying and the other half moping on my sofa – I'm actually sick of drawing him. He says he'll come to the opening but I won't hold my breath. Right must dash. I think more roses have arrived!

(Transition music: 'Clean Water' by Sleeping at Last.)

Act 2, Scene 6

Berlin school lodgings. **Jo** *enters with her suitcase.*

Jo (*to herself*) OK. So, Berlin is freezing. That's OK. And the college isn't actually in Berlin. That's OK too. At least I can see it. Just. The school lodgings are... absolutely fine. Quiet.

Jo *gets out a brown parcel containing stories and a letter which she looks at ruefully.*

Jo It's the perfect opportunity to start again.

The fire alarm goes off. **Dr Johann Bhaer** *runs in wearing a lab coat and goggles, waving oven mittens and with some kind of burnt offering in a cake tin. He climbs on a chair and flaps upwards where the smoke alarm must be.*

Jo Er, can I help?

Bhaer Yes please!

They flap frantically at the ceiling.

Bhaer I'm in big trouble if the fire service turns up again.

Jo *grabs her stack of stories and waves them. The alarm stops and a few pages spill onto the floor.*

Bhaer Let me.

Jo Thanks.

She tries to collect pages from him as he busily gathers them up.

Bhaer It's all the fault of the mackerel. The principles are sound but the problem with conventional ovens is that they don't allow you to use them unconventionally. In theory the heat generated by smoking the fish should help with the expansion of carbon dioxide in the cake – it all works. I should have used my lab.

Jo   You should...?

Bhaer   I've disarmed the fire alarm there. Don't tell anyone that.

Jo   I don't know anyone to tell.

Bhaer   Oh, the new teacher! Of course – I'm Dr Bhaer – Johann. I teach chemistry. Like I bake – very badly. With occasional smoke. How do you do.

Jo   Herr Doktor – I'm Jo. Are we housemates?

Bhaer   Sorry, yes. Not all my cooking is this disastrous. Want to try it?

The both sniff the cake tin.

Jo   Bit... mackerel-y?

Bhaer   I've made a really good rhubarb liqueur...

Jo   Not just now.

Bhaer   Of course real smokeries have dedicated equipment.

Jo   And a chimney. (*Ruefully, eying her stories*) But experiments, who knows where they'll lead?

Bhaer   Exactly! Tell that to the head teacher – every time I bump into her she reminds me of the value of written work and points out the fire exits. You obviously have a scientific mind.

Jo   I never even did science.

Shocked pause.

Bhaer (*gravely*) Everyone does science.

Jo   Not me. I kept a novel open under the desk.

Bhaer   I am genuinely appalled. Still, the worst students are sometimes the best teachers.

Jo   Here's hoping.

He looks at her sheaf of stories.

Bhaer   You can't be marking already.

Jo   Oh those aren't – they're nothing.

Bhaer   Don't tell me you're a writer.

Jo   I wish.

Bhaer   Can I read it?

Jo   No way – these are just some stories – they're a load of rubbish actually.

Bhaer   Says who?

Jo   Publishers. (*She holds up the letter.*) I was trying for something a bit different. But...

Bhaer   May I see?

She hands it over.

Bhaer   *(reading)* 'While the tone is literary, occasionally too much so, the stories themselves are rather far-fetched.' What does he know?

Jo   More than me.

Bhaer   Is it the first thing you've done?

Jo   I had a few stories in magazines. And a very bad novel.

Bhaer   Let me read them.

Jo   I'd be embarrassed...

Bhaer   Hey – you've experienced my baking. Let's be equal. Remember we chemistry teachers have souls that yearn for truth and beauty too.

Jo   Then you definitely shouldn't read my stuff.

Bhaer   I won't burn any more cakes for you...

Jo   Do you really want to read bad, far-fetched, failed literature?

Bhaer   You wouldn't believe how hard it is to find. Every library I go into... Go on. I'm interested. I'll let you try the mackerel.

Jo   Maybe – if you – don't judge.

Bhaer   You are talking to a man who once put real mince into mince pies to test the effect.

Jo   Wow – I'd like to see your family Christmas.

Bhaer   We don't do Christmas.

Jo   Oh – that's a shame.

Bhaer   Well – we are Jewish. You should see our Hanukkah. That's quite downbeat too. So, may I?

Jo *hands over the stories.*

Jo   Don't say you weren't warned.

(*Transition music: 'Enabling Environment' by Sleeping at Last.*)

Act 2, Scene 7

Gallery in Manhattan. **Amy** *is clearing up, exhausted after an evening of being fake.* **Laurie** *enters, slightly drunk. He takes in the pictures and the scene.*

Laurie   Is the maestra here?

Amy   Laurie! Am I glad to see you...

Laurie   Why, are the critics of Manhattan not queuing to meet the great artist?

Amy   Don't mock, Laurie. It's a disaster.

Laurie   I can see that. Every painting sold.

Amy   To colleagues of Fred at his law firm.

Laurie   Well. Who knew the law cared so much for art.

Amy   Not a single real sale to an actual dealer.

Laurie   Still, it's money.

Amy   As if that's what matters! I had to smile while they nodded over their enormous wine glasses and said things like 'striking', and then just stood and gossiped, and when they left the lawyers bought everything like I'm a charity case. I wanted to scream!

Laurie   Go ahead and scream now, I might just join you.

Laurie *throws back his head to yell.*

Amy   Laurie don't! Are you drunk?

Laurie   Not enough. Must try harder – let's grab one of those snooty waiters.

Amy   You should stop.

Laurie You should start.

Amy What's wrong with you?

Laurie Nothing, I'm finally grown up, qualified in law, a young man at the prime of his life. This is how we behave – isn't it nice?

Amy If this is the kind of man you're going to be then you should have stayed a boy.

Laurie Wish I had! Playing music all day – that was happy. What now? Who wants to listen?

Amy Well I don't suppose the traffic police in Times Square are exactly going to strike till the great Laurie Laurence plays them a tune. You might have to do some of the work. I'm going.

Laurie Quite right. There's nothing and no one of any significance left here. Go and find the lovely Fred – how's his taste in art? He seems more like the poster-of-some-daffodils type.

Amy Do you know what I honestly think of you?

Laurie Pining to be told.

Amy I despise you.

Laurie Ouch.

Amy Yes, because your real problem is that you're lazy. You say you want to be a musician but do you actually do it? There are a thousand jazz bars in this city. Are you knocking on their doors every morning, showing your face and asking for a booking?

Laurie Do go on – enjoy yourself.

Amy And you're selfish.

Laurie *I'm* selfish?

Amy   Very. All you think of is your own misery. You lean on your grandfather – which you can, because he loves you more than anything in the world, including his precious law firm – and you lean on your friends, like it's our job to give you a life of meaning. You're clever, Laurie, and you've got a nice face, but all that's worth nothing if you don't wake up to yourself. What would Jo say if she saw you like this?

Laurie   'Go away, Laurie.'

Amy   Oh. So that's it. And she...

Laurie   Has a heart of stone. We're not made for each other like you and the lovely Fred.

Amy   There's nothing wrong with Fred.

Laurie   Sure, he's perfectly... alright. It's just a strange idea of love from your mother's daughter.

Amy   We were talking about you.

Laurie   Oh yes.

Amy   Take some advice, Laurie. Love Jo all your days if you must but don't let it spoil you. Somewhere in there is a lovely man.

Amy *turns to go.*

Laurie   Maybe you should put *me* in your next exhibition.

Amy   There won't be a next exhibition.

Laurie   You're just bruised. You can't give up – not you.

Amy   I won't. Maybe I'm not destined to be the great painter, but I'll keep trying till I find something. I won't give up on myself. Bye, Laurie.

Amy *goes.* **Laurie** *looks after her.*

(*Transition music: 'Ill-Equipped' by Sleeping at Last.*)

Act 2, Scene 8

Berlin school lodgings. **Jo** *and* **Bhaer**.

Bhaer Congratulations! This calls for the rhubarb liqueur.

Jo It's no big deal.

Bhaer It is in this school – I've been working here three years without a compliment from the head.

Jo It's the students who won the prizes.

Bhaer Taught by you. To your success!

Jo If it is mine.

They toast. Wow.

Jo Mmm... Good flavour, a tiny bit sharp...

Bhaer Don't judge yet – the aftertaste picks up.

It does! He brings out **Jo**'s *stories.*

Bhaer Now...

Jo I'm tired – no dissections tonight.

Bhaer If not now, when?

Jo *sits reluctantly.*

Jo Alright. I'm ready.

Bhaer The language is great, the romance is fresh, and the tragedy is... pretty thrilling really.

Jo I know. They're rubbish.

Bhaer Well I'm only a humble scientist but I like your writing. I don't think it's rubbish.

Jo Herr Doktor—

He tries to tidy himself up.

Jo What?

Bhaer You only call me Herr Doktor when I'm looking dishevelled. How's that?

Jo Johann. I know they're nothing much, but I don't know how to do better.

Bhaer What would happen if you wrote for yourself?

Jo No one would want it.

Bhaer You don't know that.

Jo The only kind of power my stories ever had is what they turned into – 'The Solitary Phantom' put a carpet on my mother's bedroom floor, 'Winter's Daughter' painted my sister's nursery.

Bhaer Well, I've made some bad cakes in my time, but generally I try to learn from where I go wrong. One day I still believe I'll make the perfect gâteau.

Jo I hope I'm there when you do.

Bhaer I hope so too.

Awkward pause.

Bhaer I wonder if all your stories need is... science!

Jo   I knew you were going to say that!

Bhaer   But science shows the magic in real things.

Jo   That's not what I learned at school.

Bhaer   You were reading fantasy, remember. You didn't pay attention when they explained how petrol comes out of the ground and gets transformed into a plastic table. If you put that in a story, I bet you'd make someone wave a magic wand.

Jo   Maybe.

Bhaer   Science is full of ordinary mysteries – you flick a switch on the wall and light appears.

Jo   I know what science is. It's *not* being able to remember the periodic table, or which molecules go together to make what, and how the smallest thing is an atom but, oh whoops – no, there's something smaller, but no one agrees how it works.

Bhaer   This is what you've got completely skewed, science isn't knowledge, it's method.

Jo   That's a cop-out.

Bhaer   Wrong! How we know what we know all comes from how we ask questions. We make experiments and we don't know what the answers will be – we're humble in the face of a mystery – because we want to find out and we don't know. Not knowing is the key, it's the first brilliant thing. Accept that and everything is possible. That's the origin of explosions in my lab.

Jo   Hang on – explosions in the lab are things going awry.

Bhaer   Wrong again! Explosions, experiments, finding ways to test your ideas, this is central to the whole field! Plus, there are no mistakes if you have a working fire extinguisher. This is science – this is why real things are exciting. This the head teacher will never understand but you should, Jo, you've got imagination.

Jo   Alright. Teach me.

Bhaer   Chemistry?

Jo   Yes. I warn you; I am a terrible student.

Bhaer   I accept the challenge.

Jo   And if you succeed, come to ours for Christmas and we'll teach you about mad and festive fun.

Bhaer   Really?

Jo   Yup. The whole thing – tree, trimmings, presents, arguments.

Bhaer   It's a deal.

Jo   One thing though. If I become your student, do I get to do experiments – real ones, not like in school? I mean, where things may actually explode?

Bhaer   Definitely.

Jo   Come on then.

Bhaer   Now?

Jo (*mimicking him*) If not now, when?

Bhaer   It's the middle of the night.

Jo   Then like all seekers after truth, we shall proceed under cover of darkness!

They go. (Transition music: 'Them' by Nils Frahm.)

Act 2, Scene 9

The March family living room. **Ma** *sits on the sofa beside* **Beth**, *who is covered by a rug.*

Ma   (*to Michael*) A fox got in at the coop, Michael. I heard it and I thought I'd managed to scare it off – I put some old wire across the hole and wedged it in with a bit of wood but it's ramshackle, it won't hold. Then I saw the specks of blood. The fox must have tried to pull the bird through, she was hardly moving, chest all fluttering. Still living though. I sat on the coop in my nightie with her in my lap, stroking the silky green-black feathers. I didn't want to put something so lovely in the ground. In the morning, I dug a hole under the tree. I told Beth there'd been a fox but I'd mended it. She didn't ask about the hens. She didn't say anything. Her hands are cold. Her wrists are swollen. It's time, Michael. It's time to call our girls home.

Act 2, Scene 10

The March family living room. **Beth** *and* **Ma**, *as before. It's late. Perhaps* **Ma** *is resting.* **Jo** *enters.*

Ma   Darling.

Jo   How is she?

Ma   Very poorly.

Jo   You should rest now I'm here. Where's Meg?

Ma   She had to go – Daisy wouldn't take a bottle.

Jo   Amy?

Ma   Meg's going to speak to her.

Jo   (*to* **Beth**) Wake up Beth...

Ma   She's in a lot of pain.

Jo   Why isn't she in hospital? There must be something they can do—

Ma   She was. There isn't.

Jo   But if she's so sick—

Ma   They wanted to keep her in, they said they could give her morphine – *I* can give her morphine. If they can't keep her alive then they can't keep her.

Jo   Oh Ma...

Ma   She kept saying, take me home, Ma, how long till I go home. I thought, what are all the needles and tubes even for any more. She's my daughter – I brought her into the world and I will be the one to see her out.

Jo   I can't accept this.

Ma   I'm so sorry my darling. If she wakes, you should make the most of the time.

Jo   She's nineteen.

Ma   Then she needs our help all the more.

Jo   Does she know?

Ma   I tried to keep it from her. She saw through me.

Jo   Why didn't you tell me Ma?

Ma   Beth wanted it that way. And I wanted to spare you pain.

Jo   I'm not spared now.

Beth *stirs.*

Ma   Have some time sweetheart.

Ma *goes.*

Jo   Beth.

Beth   You came.

Jo   What can I do?

Beth   Stay.

Jo   I would never have gone if I'd known. Why didn't you tell me?

Beth   If you'd stayed, I wouldn't have had your stories. See, I was being selfish.

Jo   You're not very good at it.

Beth   Look after Ma, won't you?

Jo   I don't really want you to say things like that.

Beth   I have to.

Jo   You don't.

Beth   Try to understand.

Jo   I can't understand this.

Beth   It's like a tide. You don't notice it turn, but when it does, it can't be stopped.

Jo   You don't know that.

Beth   I do. I've known a long time, Jo. I'm not like the rest of you. I never made plans for the future. I couldn't seem to imagine it. I just never wanted to go away. The hardest part of this is leaving you. I'm not afraid, but it seems as if I would be homesick for you even in heaven.

Jo   Please don't.

Beth   I'm so tired of fighting it. I think the tide would go out easy if you'd just... tell me a story.

Jo *joins* **Beth** *on the couch. They cuddle up.*

Jo   Once there were four sisters, and the best of them was the quietest.

Beth   You can't say that—

Jo   If I'm doing the telling I can say what I like. The eldest was tall and pretty and loved nice things and always knew the kind words others needed to hear. The youngest was artistic and ambitious and just a tiny touch on the selfish side.

Beth   You'll make me laugh and laughing hurts.

Jo   Then there was the gangly misfit —

Beth   You're not.

Jo   Spotted me, though, didn't you? And then there was the one they called Mouse. And she was the best of them.

Beth   That's not true.

Jo   It's my story. Their mother despaired of what would become of her difficult brood, and their father—

Beth   They had a father?

Jo   They did.

Beth   Don't stop.

Jo   Their father had to go away. Their mother worked all the hours God sent, and still they didn't have a penny and there were no presents for Christmas that year. But Mouse sat before the hearth and said, we've got each other, and the four young faces brightened at the cheerful words, while December snow fell quietly outside and the fire crackled within. When their mother came, she brought a letter – 'Kiss all my dear girls,' their father wrote, 'especially my Beth.'

Beth *is slipping away.*

Jo   'Tell them to look after each other, shoulder their burdens womanfully, and fight their bosom enemies courageously so I may be even prouder than I already am of my little women.' Beth?

Beth *doesn't respond. It's dawn: she is gone. As transition music plays ('Flower' by Sleeping at Last)* **Beth** *leaves the stage, pausing to take a last and longing look at her sister.*

Act 2, Scene 11

Beth's funeral. **Ma** *holds a light, as do the others.* **Laurie** *is with* **Amy**, **Meg** *with* **Brooke**, **Jo** *on her own.*

Ma   A birth is a small, everyday miracle. One person becomes two – sometimes more. All that promise and hope and fear and love wrapped up in the tiniest person in the room. Someone who doesn't know we exist. While for us, a world without this small, demanding scrap of life is suddenly unimaginable. Beth entered the world surrounded by love, and that's how she left it. She had no idea of how her presence lightened our lives. All Beth ever wanted was to be close to the ones she loved.

Weren't we the lucky ones? Now we have to carry her with us, because we're still here. Her life, and what it meant to us, is the gift she leaves.

Ma *and the girls place their lights at the far end of the traverse, where we imagine* **Beth***'s coffin to be. Each girl hugs* **Ma** *in turn.* **Amy** *returns to* **Laurie** *and they hold each other. There's a moment when* **Jo** *sees this, and takes it on board. (Transition music: 'Atlantic' by Sleeping at Last.)*

Act 2, Scene 12

The March family living room. **Ma** *is asleep on the sofa, the box* **Beth** *once gave to* **Jo** *beside her.* **Jo** *enters, trying not to wake* **Ma** *– but fails.*

Ma   Jo, where were you?

Jo   Out walking.

Ma   Come and sit.

Jo *does so, reluctantly.*

Ma   I worry.

Jo   I don't want to be a burden to you.

Ma   You're not a burden, you're a daughter. Sometimes it looks the same thing but it's not. (*Indicating the box*) Remember this?

Jo   Beth made it.

Ma   And you filled it. Some of your old stories were in here, I had a little read.

Act 2

Jo   I wrote those years ago.

Ma   They're funny, some of them. No wonder Beth loved them.

Jo   Did she?

Ma   The box was under her bed. Why don't you write? It always used to take you out of yourself.

Jo   Nothing comes.

Ma   That's because you don't let it. If you're not pacing your room you're pacing the streets. Grief needs a day off.

Jo   It's the loneliness, Ma.

Ma   I know.

Jo   It's not as if anyone likes what I write.

Ma   So what. Write for yourself.

Jo   What's the point of something no one will ever see.

Ma   I don't know. But I do know you're happiest when you write. Have a look through.

Pause.

Ma   Write something for me.

Jo   Maybe.

Ma   Jo, I'm sorry I didn't tell you. About Beth.

Jo   I understand Ma.

Ma   All the same. I am sorry.

They hug. **Ma** *gets up, placing the box open on the table where* **Jo** *can see it.*

Ma   Goodnight.

*Ma goes. **Jo** tries to avoid looking at the box, but eventually she approaches the table and sits down. Music plays (song performed on stage by **Laurie** with guitar is 'South' by Sleeping at Last) as **Jo** opens the box and begins to read its contents.*

Beth *enters unseen by **Jo** and watches her for a moment before putting **Jo**'s scarlet writing hat in the box. **Jo**, reaching into the box for a pen, discovers the hat there and puts it on. She takes out a pen and begins to scribble on a story. **Beth** smiles and goes.*

Act 2, Scene 13

*The March family living room. **Amy** is taping up cardboard boxes. **Laurie** enters.*

Laurie   These the last ones?

Amy   Yup.

Laurie   Promise?

Amy   I'll be there in a minute.

*They kiss. **Laurie** takes a box and goes. **Amy** is looking at her old home as **Jo** enters.*

Jo   Ready?

Amy   Sure.

Jo   Amy?

Amy   Sort of. Not really.

Jo   You can do it.

Amy   Been dreaming about it practically all my life. Now it comes, I don't know what to do with myself.

Jo   You're not going far.

Amy   I'm going down the road! It feels like forever and very far away.

Jo   Home will still be here.

Amy   It's different, since Beth.

Jo   I know.

Amy   It all happened here.

Jo   Come on, smile little sister. It's going to be amazing, look what you're doing with your life – your own pop-up gallery, making a new home. You've even turned Laurie into a useful citizen – I could never do that.

Amy   Yeah...

Jo   My sister, the entrepreneur.

Amy (*upset*) Feels like I'm abandoning you.

Jo   Oh Amy, you're not. You have every right to make your life. God – me telling you that!

Amy   But will you be alright?

Jo   If I'm not I'll come and shout at you.

Amy   I would actually like that.

Jo   Look into my eyes Amy: I am OK. All those years arguing over who gets to lie on the sofa and now I can't get rid of you.

Amy   Will you ring if you need to?

Jo   Yes.

Amy   You can come round whenever.

Jo   You'll be sick of the sight of me.

Amy   Goes without saying.

Jo *picks up the last box.*

Jo   Right.

Amy   Right.

Jo   Last one out is a loser.

Amy   What – wait!

They go.

Act 2, Scene 14

The March family living room: Christmas Eve. Music plays (transition song performed by **Laurie** *with guitar in mischievous, upbeat style and tempo is Bing Crosby's 'I'll Be Home for Christmas') as the scene is set by the cast, who bring in a long trestle table and lay it up for a feast, adding decorations, the Christmas wishes box and a family photograph. As the music ends,* **Meg** *enters in a coat with a box of food.*

Meg   (*calls*) Jo! (*To herself*) As if.

Meg *writes something and puts it in the wishes box. She takes in the family photograph.* **Amy** *enters, also in a coat, with a box of Christmas supplies.*

Amy   I got the veg – Laurie's bringing the booze. Oh...

She takes in the photograph. The sisters have a moment together.

Amy   I wish Ma didn't have to work today.

Meg   We'll make it good for her.

Amy   Any sign of Jo?

Meg   What do you think? Have you put a wish in the box?

Amy   I'll write one now.

While **Amy** *writes her wish,* **Jo** *enters with shopping bags.*

Jo   Happy Christmas ladies!

Meg   Jo...

Amy   Have you wrapped *anything*?

Jo   No – and I'm not going to – I've made a world-changing discovery.

Meg   Which is?

Jo *takes out ready-wrapped presents.*

Jo   If you go to the right shops, other people do it for you. There.

Meg   Have you got any money left?

Jo   No fretting – it's Christmas.

Meg   You should save something for a rainy day.

Jo *doesn't plan on taking this sensible advice.*

Amy (*to* **Jo**) What time is your friend coming?

Meg   Brooke's bringing him from the station.

Amy   Looking forward to meeting him...

Meg   He sounded really nice on the phone.

Jo   Don't.

Meg   What?

Jo Act like a pair of matrons.

Amy We're not!

Jo Just because I've got a male friend coming over doesn't mean I'm about to marry him. I haven't even seen him in ages.

Meg Sure.

Jo He's just a colleague.

Meg Of course he is. That's fine.

Amy A colleague you've invited for *Christmas*...

Meg Amy... (*To* **Jo**) Have you put a wish in the box?

Jo Not yet.

Jo *takes in the photograph. It's hard to write a wish this year.*

Meg Has anyone tackled the lights?

Jo I'll do it.

Meg *and* **Amy** *busy themselves decorating the room.* **Jo** *tries the lights: they don't work.*

Jo Perfect.

Laurie *enters carrying bottles and a newspaper, followed by* **Brooke** *and* **Bhaer** *bearing gifts.*

Laurie Delivery!

Brooke Sssh—

Laurie Sorry...

Brooke The twins are sleeping in the hall, Meg.

Laurie *holds out the newspaper to* **Meg** *with a wink.*

Jo You made it.

Bhaer A deal's a deal.

Everyone is annoyingly interested in how **Jo** *and* **Bhaer** *will greet each other. It's an understated kiss on the cheek.*

Amy Well hello, Johann.

Jo This is my sister, Amy.

Amy Nice to meet you.

Bhaer Likewise – and you're Meg?

Meg Happy Christmas – hope you're ready for this.

Bhaer Can't wait – should these go under the tree?

He hands over a bag of presents.

Jo You shouldn't have.

Bhaer Berlin has a great Christmas market.

Laurie Lights not working?

Meg They're a law unto themselves. They're switched on...

Laurie *unscrews random bulbs to see which is breaking the circuit – no luck – as* **Jo** *sits with* **Bhaer** *on the sofa. While they talk, Meg shows the newspaper around surreptitiously.*

Jo How've you been?

Bhaer Good. Busy. I read your book.

Jo Uh-oh – time for another dissection?

Bhaer Yes – brilliant. Funny. Sad. Beautiful.

Jo Thank you Herr Doktor.

He smartens himself up.

Bhaer   Better?

Laurie *and* **Amy** *launch themselves onto the sofa either side of* **Jo** *and* **Bhaer**.

Amy   Anything interesting in the paper, Laurie?

Laurie   Not much.

Amy   Not even in the Christmas books section?

Laurie   Oh, as it happens the top picks do make for a fascinating read.

Meg   What's number one in the best books for Christmas, Laurie?

Brooke   Hey – I don't suppose you could read it to us?

Jo   Let me see that!

Jo *scrambles for the newspaper and gets it.*

Jo   (*reading*) 'A true synthesis of ideas and feeling, embodied in vivid character and compelling prose. The story is leavened by a humour that brings it charmingly alive. The work of a born storyteller.'

Laurie   That's you by the way, Jo March.

Jo   That's incredible.

Laurie   Isn't it?

Brooke   Every word true.

Laurie   If Brooke says that you can rely on it.

Amy   It's going to sell like hot cakes.

Meg   You deserve this.

Jo   I can't take it in.

Ma *enters, taking in the sight of them crowded over the sofa.*

Ma   What a sight! That sofa won't last another day.

Amy   Jo's book got chosen as the best Christmas read!

Meg   There's a whole thing about it in the newspaper.

Ma   Let me see – would you look at that!

Ma *hugs* **Jo.**

Jo   I can't believe it.

Ma   I can. Enjoy it darling.

Meg   Let me take your bag.

Ma   I should write my notes before I forget everything—

Jo   No!

Amy   I'll get the whiskey.

Jo   Hide the bag Meg – Ma, we've got a guest.

Bhaer   Mrs March, nice to meet you.

Ma   Johann, I hope my girls are looking after you.

Amy   We're doing a fantastic job.

Jo   Ma, what's the haul?

Ma   Lovely little nine pounder, one sevener, and a dear little girl of five pounds four ounces. The parents are so young and so in love with her.

Amy   Let's do our toast – induct these boys into the proper March Christmas Eve.

Jo   I haven't done mine...

Meg   I'll get some paper.

Amy   Johann, this is a March Christmas tradition.

Bhaer   You'll have to tell me what to do.

Amy   Write down a wish – it can be anything, even just a hope.

Jo   The trick is not to think too hard – write down the first thing that comes.

They do.

Bhaer   Do we read them out?

Amy   They go to the master of ceremonies which this year is—

Meg   Me, Amy...

Amy *gathers the wishes and gives them to* **Meg**, *who has the box.*

Meg   First, there's one wish that won't be here this year, and Johann you won't know to miss it but we will. And we know what it would have said, because it always said the same thing.

Amy   Apart from the year she made us give away our dinner.

Ma   Never to be forgotten.

Meg   So, to be grateful to have each other. Beth.

They toast **Beth**.

Meg   So. On. To find a sleep routine that actually works on the twins—

Jo   Meg.

Meg   —*and* put the washing on before it starts coming out the top of the basket.

Laurie Brooke.

Meg To scour London for artists who don't have a bean and no one knows they exist and make sure their talent has a chance to flourish.

Ma Amy, that's a lovely thing.

Meg To write a book called *The Magic of Reality* that makes people love science.

Brooke I'd read it.

Jo Johann – really?

Ma Heaven help us...

Meg To make more time for my sisters, and learn how to leave the house in under an hour.

Amy Meggie.

Meg That's me... To work less and spend more time with my babies, and their babies.

Ma Guilty.

Meg This one's big. To ask Amy to marry me, again.

Laurie *adopts a dramatic proposal pose.*

Laurie What do you say?

Amy We'll discuss that later.

Meg Now who can this be – to begin a new story.

Ma Jo.

The lights flicker on. The space is full of light.

Jo   Magic!

Bhaer   Science will have done that.

Meg   Dear Mad Marches, and friends, I give you, a *good* Christmas.

They toast. Outro music ('Atlantic' by Sleeping at Last) rises over the voices of the family and friends as they chatter together for a few moments.

Blackout.

Acknowledgements

Marking *Little Women*'s 150th anniversary by adapting it for the stage in a modern British setting was the brilliant idea of Grace Chapman at The Space theatre. Throughout the process she played a key role as dramaturge, and both I and this adaptation owe so much to her skill and insight - as well as to her ability to make restructuring and other painful textual surgery sound somehow doable and even exciting.

We were lucky enough to be able to bring our director, Sepy Baghaei, and key members of the cast into the theatre during the writing process. Their improvisations helped us find ways to tell the story in a contemporary setting. Almost as importantly, the cast and Sepy were huge fun to work with, something that also found its way into the adaptation.

No list of thanks would be complete without mentioning Adam Hemming, artistic director at The Space, whose generosity, kindness, and ability to bring together and nurture new artists are legendary to all who've worked with him. My thanks to him and to all at The Space.

LITTLE WOMEN

Production Note

Other than the single, loved, slightly-worn sofa that anchors the March family's life, everything in terms of props and set should be portable, coming and going with a swiftness that mirrors the changes and growth in the sisters.

The original production was set in the traverse, allowing the audience to feel a part of the March family's living room. Cast sat at the sides, bringing any props with them to enable maximum pace and fluency.

Transition music from the original production is suggested in brackets, as are two songs that were performed live at key moments in the story by the actor-musician playing Laurie.

First Performance

The first performance of *Little Women* was at The Space from 27 November to 15 December 2018 with the following cast:

Meg March – Isabel Crowe

Amy March – Stephanie Dickson

Jo March – Amy Gough

Dr Bhaer – Jonathan Hawkins

Beth March – Miranda Horn

Ma March – Victoria Jeffrey/Rachael Claye

Laurie Laurence – Sean Stevenson
Brooke – Joshua Stretton

Director and sound design – Sepy Baghaei

Producer and dramaturge – Grace Chapman

Lighting – Andy Straw
Costume design – Kelli Baleta

The Space is a performing arts centre based in a converted church on the Isle of Dogs, East London. Space Productions is their home-grown professional theatre company. Find out more at space.org.uk

For performance rights, please contact rclaye@me.com